KELLI MARÍA KORDUCKI

HARD TO DO

THE SURPRISING, FEMINIST HISTORY OF BREAKING UP

COACH HOUSE BOOKS, TORONTO

first edition

 Canada Council **Conseil des Arts**
for the Arts **du Canada**

 ONTARIO ARTS COUNCIL
CONSEIL DES ARTS DE L'ONTARIO
an Ontario government agency
un organisme du gouvernement de l'Ontario

 Canadä

Published with the generous assistance of the Canada Council for the
Arts and the Ontario Arts Council. Coach House Books also gratefully
acknowledges the support of the Government of Canada through the
Canada Book Fund and the Government of Ontario through the Ontario
Book Publishing Tax Credit.

LIBRARY AND ARCHIVES CANADA CATALOGUING IN PUBLICATION

Korducki, Kelli María, author
        Hard to do : the surprising, feminist history of breaking up / Kelli
María Korducki.

Issued in print and electronic formats.
ISBN 978-1-55245-352-0 (softcover).

        1. Separation (Psychology). 2. Interpersonal relations. 3. Love.
I. Title.

HQ801.K66 2018   306.89   C2017-905080-X
                                                      C2017-905081-8

Hard To Do is available as an ebook: ISBN 978 1 77056 527 2 (PDF), ISBN 978
1 77056 526 5 (EPUB).

For my mother

Introduction

In the year I broke up with someone I had loved and lived with for nearly a decade, I attended four weddings over a period of six weeks. This fluke of timing belied a cosmic indifference that felt so on-the-nose, I couldn't help but laugh. How funny it was to come out of a nine-year relationship at twenty-eight, I thought, and to start all over at the precise moment when everyone around me was choosing 'shit' over 'get off the pot.' How hilarious to get sloppily drunk and dance all night in celebration of forever-love when the evidence suggests you'll die alone. I laughed at all of it, the animatronic caw of a person whose muscle memory has unlearned, over a course of months, passable vocalizations for joy.

I'd spent my twenties watching girlfriends date their way through a succession of assholes, slackers, softboys, and duds, before eventually landing on lovely people who did not meet those descriptors and settling down with them. I'd gone the other way and gotten serious fast with a kind, brainy housemate at the beginning of my second year of university, functionally a hausfrau before I'd even exited my teens. The messy trial-and-error of a dating phase was something I'd escaped, perhaps unfairly, and I wondered at the time whether my lucky roll of the dice had clouded my perception of the actual odds against what I seemed to have won.

My relationship ended for any number of reasons, but a dearth of affection wasn't one of them. I was unhappy for reasons that felt trivial when I said them out loud, which was almost never; I barely had the language to describe my predicament in the first place. More than anything else, my uncertainty manifested as a physical sensation, a gut-level insistence I no longer had the option to ignore. I was privileged enough to recognize a value in my own happiness and the integrity in making a sacrifice to achieve it. I also knew that to do otherwise would be, at the act's core, a selfishness of its own.

The truth was that my on-paper reasons were there, and they still make sense after the fact. The timing was bad, for one. My dreams for myself were bigger, louder, more insistent than my dreams for an us – any us, even hypothetical pairings that would never exist. I was ambivalent about marriage, period, and about children even more so. I'd just put in an IUD that I vowed not to remove until it expired in my mid-thirties. Above all, there was too much I wanted to do, too many windows that my sanity demanded I keep open. The trappings of permanence made me feel uneasy, and for years youth had let me push them away, until the day it abruptly stopped being enough.

The relationship might not have ended at all if I'd been born even a generation earlier. The kind of life I wanted lacked precedent among the women who had shaped me, by their own choice but also by their more limited options. I didn't have much money and my professional prospects were limited within a dying industry of ideas and words. Yet I intrinsically grasped that my life could be an adventure of my own making; this seedling of a vision felt too precious to set aside, even as it rendered my heart ugly and wrong. I suspected that nobody in my family understood, nor anyone in his. I steeled myself to be hated.

That summer, during the worst of it, I paced outside a Chicago McDonald's while waiting for a train to cart me home from a music festival whose details the anguish of that period has all but erased. The July heat was oppressive, just like everything else.

My father was to pick me up from the train station in Milwaukee, my hometown some two hours away, where I was hauling my corpse for an annual summer visit. In the shadow of the McDonald's sign, I phoned him my whereabouts. On the other end of the line he sounded almost as deflated as I felt. My grandfather was slowing down, he said. His memory wasn't so good. His heart, even worse. My father's pained resignation to his own father's mortality was taking a toll, despite the distributed support of a half-dozen siblings and my mother, his wife of thirty-four years. I thought about how, in thirty-four years, I would be five years older than my father was at that moment. I thought about how, one day, much sooner, he would be old, too.

'Life is hard,' he said, pointedly, 'and harder if you're alone.' Don't make a decision you'll regret for the rest of your life, he added. Or maybe I'd inferred it.

Life *is* hard, and all the harder because of decisions like the one I ultimately made: to walk away from a sure thing. Nuts! Pause for a moment to consider the tremendous novelty of that choice within a society whose institutions continue to uphold the nuclear family as its foundation. The primacy of personal growth and self-actualization over-rides consideration of the collective yet counterintuitively sets us up to risk thwarting our own self-interest – that is, it sets us up to do what we want in the moment. And so, this terrifying leap I ultimately made was the only thing I could talk about for many months, daring anyone at all to talk some sense into my hungover husk.

Today, we have the liberty to step away from relationships, to start over. It's a licence many of us may not even think of as a freedom, having gulped our first breaths knowing in our bones that we exist to follow our bliss. Don't know what your bliss is? Fake it 'til you make it – the late-capitalist mantra that's arguably the central proverb of contemporary wisdom.

It seems almost retrograde to regard individual relationships as critical pivots in the grand scheme of our self-propelled stories. It's unlikely you'll be denied a job – let alone locked up – on account of a domestic partnership not working out, and yet both scenarios have happened to Western women within the past century. As of the 1970s, we no longer have to prove mistreatment in order to obtain a divorce, and we don't even need to marry in the first place. It's taken for granted that a majority of us will form multiple romantic partnerships over our lifetimes.

And yet, we agonize over our cultivation of meaningful human connection. We make couple selfies our avatars on Facebook and instagram our friend groups with the zeal of paparazzi. Our intimate freedoms are startlingly new, and they absorb us in exhilarating pursuit. But the basic blueprint of Western partnership – a marriage between two people until one or the other is dead – remains tethered to a time that was not so free, nor so distant. Our grandmothers' mothers were not likely able to own property, to economically support themselves, or to vote. For my contemporaries plumbing the uneasy depths of semi-young adulthood, the burden of history hangs in balance with the tightly bundled load of our personal needs and desires. The archetype of successful adulthood still rests on finding our 'other half.'

The person with whom I broke up those years ago was (and is) kind, sweet, smart, and good. The dictionary definition of a mensch, he also made (and, as far as I can guess, continues to make) much more money than I do. I adored his family and knew that, even after the months and years that would inevitably pass, I would continue to miss them; they had become my family, too. It felt cruel that I had been raised with a set of expectations about partnership that would make this terrible outcome also, ironically, the one that was best for everyone.

That gruesome irony is what this book endeavours to unpack. I wanted to get to the bottom of the cultural and economic developments that have enabled women like me to break up with stable and decent partners, or with any partners at all – and why, despite those developments, the decision to stay or go has remained so charged. When did it become so damn difficult to figure out not only what we *should* want, but what we *do* want? I wanted to understand where in history the material concerns and emotional ethics of partnership has diverged in the first place – where and how it had become impolite to mention money and love in the same breath, as though their symbiotic relationship isn't gleefully reinforced by holidays that celebrate consumption or karat counts on rings.

The road to our status quo was paved by history's haves. Marriage was about the allocation of stuff, and its backstory is a timeline of wealth-preserving demands by white, property-owning members of Western society. In many respects, our love lives continue to be governed on a presumption of heteronormativity, whiteness, and material comforts.

Romantic love in long-term partnership was, itself, invented alongside the market economy. The partner choices we have as women and femmes of any sexual orientation are a direct inheritance of the conditional freedoms we have gained as a by-product of capitalism, made ambiguous by the inequalities that this system continues to reinforce. My generation of women and femmes might be the first with the unlucky privilege to weigh the contradictions of an ideal partnership and choose outside the conventions of shared wisdom. We are, whether we like it or not, pioneers. What do we do with this mantle we've inherited?

For those of us who are not straight-leaning, who are not gender-conforming, who have crossed the threshold of middle age in the absence of a partner, this question probably feels a bit dull. The heteronormative rites of middle- and upper-class adulthood are small existential potatoes, all in all. But never before in history have we demanded so much of our significant others, such complex criteria along social, economic, emotional, and sexual lines. To complicate existence even further, the parameters of an ideal life have never been less clear. It's hard to know what we want when the potential stakes are higher than we might want to admit. And despite the widely accepted notion that personal happiness is paramount above most other things, the liberty to accept this as truth is so new that it isn't always apparent when we do or don't have it.

Just as the flaws of past relationships become clear once viewed with the wisdom of hindsight, the developments throughout history that have allowed for men, women, and everyone in between to have some semblance of romantic freedom seem obvious when traced backwards from the now. Nothing is natural. We are a pragmatic species. At the same time, these bread-crumb paths through the forest of our past aren't necessarily the ones we might have guessed. This book is a forensic investigation of the material conditions that have led us, particularly as women, to the present moment – the political, religious, and economic shifts that have made breaking up possible, yet still so hard to do.

1

Leaving a Good Man™

Several years ago, in the immediate aftermath of the prolonged and heart-wrenching breakup that persisted in destroying my entire life over the course of many months, a friend sent me an essay she thought I should read. She was also in the middle of a breakup – a divorce – and we had met a few years earlier through the partners we were simultaneously losing. As one terrible summer faded into an even bleaker fall, we became Gchat pen pals in an ongoing correspondence of mutual despair.

I was officially single and deeply ashamed. To me, my breakup had constituted a karmic injustice that I could have stopped – against my wonderful former partner, against our respective families, and against the scores of women throughout history who'd been denied the love and respect of a Good Man. My friend told me she looked at this must-read piece from time to time, whenever she was feeling scared about the future. I still wasn't sure that I might have one.

Go, even though you love him.

Go, even though he's kind and faithful and dear to you.

Go, even though he's your best friend and you're his.

Go, even though you can't imagine your life without him.

Go, even though he adores you and your leaving will devastate him.

Go, even though your friends will be disappointed or surprised or pissed off or all three.

Go, even though you once said you would stay.

Go, even though you're afraid of being alone.

> Go, even though you're sure no one will ever love you as
> well as he does.
> Go, even though there is nowhere to go.
> Go, even though you don't know exactly why you can't stay.
> Go, because you want to.
> Because wanting to leave is enough.

She copy-pasted the excerpt into the chat window so that I might read it first, a block of beatitudes for the guilty heart. The piece, 'The Truth That Lives There,' was actually an entry in an ongoing advice column, answered by a then-anonymous woman addressed only as Dear Sugar.

On the other end were a series of women seeking answers, all with versions of the same problem. 'Dear Sugar,' the first wrote, and proceeded to describe her age (twenty-six), her new husband (older; kind and funny), his wedding proposal (like something out of a movie starring Audrey Hepburn). 'I do love him,' the woman insisted. 'And yet … I want to leave but I'm also terrified of hurting my husband, who has been so good to me and who I consider my best friend,' she pleaded. 'Sugar, please help me.' Signed, Playing it Safe.

There were four other letters like it, grouped together. Signed, Standing Still. Signed, Claustrophobic. Signed, Leaving a Marriage. Signed, Trying. 'Trying is lying,' my therapist had said, months earlier, when I realized it was over.

Sugar replied to the collective because, as she explained it, their letters told a story complete enough to answer themselves. They brought her back to a painful moment of her own life – 'the most painful,' she wrote. She'd married at nineteen and divorced her Good Man after a fistful of ambivalent, yet deeply love-filled years. Why ambivalent?

Even the all-knowing oracle couldn't answer. Youth was almost certainly a culprit. Class hang-ups, too, and not as much mutual compatibility as there had once seemed. Moreover, wrote Sugar, she left because she had to.

'Certainly, an ethical and evolved life entails a whole lot of doing things one doesn't particularly want to do and not doing things one very much does, regardless of gender,' she wrote. 'But an ethical and evolved life also entails telling the truth about oneself and living out that truth.' She shared her suspicion that doing what one wants to do seems a particularly difficult prospect for women. As I read, I imagined an alternate plane of existence, where some version of me slammed shut my laptop and flung it at the wall.

This column from the then-anonymous Sugar had been written by Cheryl Strayed, about a year before she'd unmasked herself and released the bestselling 2012 memoir *Wild: From Lost to Found on the Pacific Crest Trail. Wild* is a chronicle of dissolution: the death of a parent, the destruction of a marriage, a stint at addiction, and the author's self-redemption by way of a gruelling physical quest. Throughout, Strayed offers a narrative trajectory that might sound familiar to the unhappy women plaintively seeking answers to counterintuitive romantic predicaments from advice columns, Reddit boards, and the stereotypically pinker quadrants of the internet.

In *Wild*, Strayed encounters marital demise as the consequence of crisis, the final punctuating snap after a tailspin in the years immediately after her mother's death. The trauma of her grief, of her life, renders her crazy; it is *crazy* to push away a Good Man. The advice column offers a condensed version of this narrative, with the crazy turned down and centred, instead, on an empathic urgency. 'There was nothing wrong with my ex-husband. He wasn't perfect, but he was pretty close,' Strayed's Sugar writes. From the very beginning of their whirlwind courtship and marriage, Strayed recalls something nagging inside of her: 'a tiny clear voice that would not, no matter what I did, stop saying *go*.'

Sugar offers permission, and in it, validation that listening to one's instinct is the exact opposite of insane. There is nothing pretty or interesting, after all, in coming spectacularly undone – nor in internalizing that as your fate. It is not crazy to leave even a good man, and it will not ruin you.

I've long suspected that women subconsciously accept some version of the belief that we're supposed to want secure romantic relationships more than anything in the world. The logical extension of that is an expectation that we should want to stay, to make it work, the moment we find ourselves with a partner who is decent and willing. It's still a broadly accepted facet of collective pseudoscience that while men are biologically compelled to spread their seed, we women are wired to be bond-formers, family-builders, nature's natural nurturers.

You could say that our cultural understanding of women's autonomy isn't totally in sync with the logistics of twenty-first-century partnership, and the internet would appear to agree. A 2015 thread on Reddit's TwoXChromosomes board opens with a PSA: 'You can break up with someone for any reason, or for no reason at all,' it reads. 'You don't have to have a "good reason" to end a relationship.'

Posting under the handle MissPredicament, the page's writer muses over the observation that an astonishing number of women in Reddit's relationships forum seem to be mired in the same existential conundrum. They are unhappy in relationships that don't really have anything wrong with them. 'I wish someone had told me when I was much younger that I didn't have to have an airtight legal case for a breakup – all I had to have was a desire to no longer be in that relationship,' she writes. 'I would have saved myself a lot of time.' The post received over a thousand replies.

There are others like it. 'Have you ever broken up with a good guy? Or have you ever broken up with a good girl?' reads one, on Reddit's AskWomen board, a plaintive call for some proof of precedent. An essay on the website HelloGiggles sketches the author's toughest breakup, with a 'nice guy' she calls Sam. She steels herself to complete the deed, only to realize that her nice guy wants to stay together. 'My guilt ran around inside me, beating every organ like a gong,' she writes.

'The problem with some guys is they're not a problem at all,' reads another essay, this time on MTV.com. When women end partnerships, it seems that the emotion we feel perhaps more acutely than the eviscerating grief of love lost is the guilt of having pushed it away.

This sub-genre of women's-advice-cum-confessional writing appears to confront what is so often perceived to be the dominant expectation of the opposite sex – that far too many men are unwilling or unable to commit to a relationship. Women and men both are raised to believe that boys will be boys and men will be scoundrels, a truism reinforced by headlines and hashtags in testament of bad male behaviour. We call it toxic masculinity, and are taught to search for a prince among all the warty frogs. In the face of perceived scarcity, opting out of a stable partnership with a good man carries a weight of ethical frivolity. Breaking up with a man who actually wants to be there, and who is good and decent, seems irresponsible at best. It's like scoring big in the lotto and torching your winnings for sport.

Of course, the perception of scarcity is just that: a perception, a myth. It is facile and essentializing to paint any gender as more or less willing than others to engage in the labour of a relationship. Yet for women who date men, in the context of a patriarchal society, life isn't short on reminders that a Good Man can be hard to find.

Despite the advice of so many personal essays and Reddit threads, the Family Relationships category of Amazon's self-help section is conspicuously short on books that speak to a woman's right to call it quits, let alone her desire to. When I looked, it appeared that even the most reasoned, professional-counsellor-authored tomes on twenty-first-century romantic dissolution hinted in some way that breakups with men were the result of fundamental brokenness: in men's behaviour, in women's selection criteria. It might not shock you to learn that there is no self-help book marketed at straight women titled *Trust Me: Lose the Nice Guy*.

There seems almost to be a tacit assumption that the heartbroken women nursing solitary bottles of wine (and yes, in the materiality of self-help cliché, the drink is always wine) are imbibing to numb the ruminations unique to falling for fuckboys – millennial shorthand for men who expect to play the field without much care for emotional repercussions.

Fuckboys are the unnamed 'you' in breakup songs from Kesha's 'Thinking of You' to Taylor Swift's 'We Are Never Ever Getting Back Together.' The 'I know you want it'–leering narrator in Robin Thicke's 'Blurred Lines' is absolutely a fuck-boy. So is Drake's judgmental and horny alter ego in 'Hotline Bling.' Fuckboys – these noncommittal charmers who want nothing but to love you and leave – are the scourge of our time, the literature seems to tell us.

But this type of man, or the conception we have of him, predates the current terminology. Throughout history, men have taken from women, of women. The Spanish conquest of Latin America is written neatly into my own DNA, a story of white men and the brown women they'd conquered. 'A cow never gives the milk away for free,' my Salvadoran mother advised me the moment I began dating, as though the only thing any boy could possibly want from me was sex. Withholding it, without regard for my own desire, was understood to be the sole bargaining chip at my disposal.

The bulk of relationship guidance aimed at women who date men is presented as some variation of a fuckboy recovery manual, which, by process of elimination, leaves the elusive Good Man as the secret to romantic success. The dynamics of communication, care, and personal agency that so heavily figure into any type of interpersonal relationship are touched upon only in service to the hypothesis that most men are trash, but you probably still want them anyway. You idiot, you.

The women in these books tend to share the burden of big hearts and low standards. In her introduction to *It's Called a Breakup Because It's Broken*, Amiira Ruotola-Behrendt (whose husband and co-author had previously co-authored the bestselling 'advice' manual *He's Just Not That Into You*) assures her female readers: 'I've been the girl who not only suffers through an unhealthy, demoralizing relationship but then goes back to it in hopes that time spent apart has inspired him to love me enough to change … or even try.'

Licenced New York City relationship counsellor Rachel Sussman admits, in her foreword to *The Breakup Bible: The Smart Woman's Guide to Healing from a Breakup or Divorce*, that her own rocky history with relationships came from having made 'decisions that weren't always in my best interest, that chipped away at my self-esteem, and that kept me in a state of suspended melancholy.' Those decisions, she goes on to imply, had to do with choosing the wrong type of partner. She writes that it wasn't until a (male) friend pulled her aside and expressed concern over her 'constant' decision to date 'toxic men when so many nice guys ask you out' that she began to re-evaluate her approach to the game of love. The book received many positive reviews, at least by Amazon users.

Even the misleadingly promising *How to Dump a Guy: A Coward's Manual* seems not to treat the endeavour of breaking up with total seriousness, inviting its would-be woman dumper to fill out a tongue-in-cheek worksheet that catalogues the dumpee's particular flaw ('e.g. Cling-on, Sexual Savant, etc.'), the '[d]ate you first realized you had to dump him,' breakup outfit, and so forth. It's as though the book's female authors viewed the exercise of ending a relationship as nothing more than a future curio to gab about, à la Carrie Bradshaw, over a three-mimosa brunch with girlfriends.

I didn't see much of my own romantic experience reflected in Amazon's recommendations. I've only dated a few men in my life, all of whom were great. Each relationship lasted at least a year; every time, I'd been the one to end it. Maybe a Good Man is hard to find, but I seem to have a knack for it.

I'm lucky though; many of the women I know can attest to some experience that validates the condescending black-and-white of self-help rationale. Many have been ghosted – dumped without word or warning by way of total silence. Others have found themselves grown attached to men who refuse monogamy, yet remain resolute in their distaste for the ethics of communication that successful polyamorous arrangements seem to be founded on.

We all know the reasons – be they stereotypes or kernels of truth – for why a woman might be inclined to fall for the 'wrong' kind of man, one who seems rakish or noncommittal. Players have an irritating tendency to make for better lovers. Maybe there's an appeal in imagining oneself as the woman who can 'tame' a fuckboy's ways – or, alternately, to have a bit of fun with them. The tropes are tired and trite, but they aren't totally wrong.

There are also plenty of unsurprising, age-old reasons for why the phenomenon of the fuckboy (or whatever we're calling him at any given moment) is one that's so unabashedly gendered. What is new, if anything, are the advances in communication and culture that have made sexual dalliances easier to come by and less of a potential liability on a person's time, psyche, or reputation. People are freer than ever before to chase their romantic whims, to indefinitely pursue whatever arbitrary combination of attributes they're sure will make them happy in the now. Prospective partners are commodities we can pick up then put back on the shelf. A warm body is only a screen-swipe away.

Yet despite today's freedoms and conveniences, men and women remain fundamentally unequal in our society.

It's common knowledge that men earn more on average than women do, even for the same types of work. Men are disproportionately represented in the upper echelons of influence and capital. They're typically bigger and stronger than women, better equipped to have and take.

And therein lies the bind. No relationship is an island. They are socio-cultural units informed by the world at large. Even the most egalitarian partnerships must negotiate the power structures that threaten to reproduce themselves, on a micro level, within every marriage and romance and bed. And because of this, the way women experience partnership cannot help but be fundamentally fraught in ways that men might never know, whether or not we admit it to ourselves.

The timeless trope of the fuckboy – the noncommittal rogue, the Casanova – is a function of the tiresome imbalance that has always existed between men and women in Western society. And in the age of internet media, it feels as though we're crescendoing toward some kind of tipping point. 'Alongside the wage gap and the emotional labour gap, the antics of softboys, f-ckboys, fading and ghosting constitute a pronounced communication gap [between men and women],' writes journalist Sarah Ratchford in a 2017 article for Canada's *Flare* magazine, citing a glossary of terms that more or less describe the same general idea. While a person needn't be male to be a challenging partner, Ratchford argues that most women are raised to be considerate of others' feelings in ways that many men simply aren't. The argument goes that this perceived communication gap – again, the result of asymmetrical ethics instilled during men's and women's respective upbringings – has produced a spate of men who altogether lack the tools necessary to be the kinds of partners that modern women want. Women who date men have, in turn, increasingly given up on the prospect of relationships altogether. It's worth mentioning that the article is titled 'Why I'm Giving Up Dating Men and Just Staying Home.'

Ratchford leans on the observation that boys are raised to value different things from girls, and that men and women are socially rewarded for different behaviours, but the emotional inattentiveness she describes seems to be less the consequence of men's conditioned inability to exercise consideration for others than their unjust possession of the upper hand – and the privilege to play it at will. Though it's certainly possible that a deficiency in empathy can account for the sexual callousness of individual men, it stands to reason that in a romantic (and literal) marketplace where they are overvalued, their bad behaviour might remain unchecked (or at least tolerated) for years.

Women, on the other hand, face a labour market that values them less than men at the outset of their careers, and goes even lower than that should they choose to begin families. This is compounded (for women who date men) by a relationship market that sees their worth rapidly deplete with the passage of time, thanks in large part to the baleful tick of our biological clock. Aspiring to gain a foothold in either marketplace threatens success in the other. In both, we're at a clear disadvantage from the start.

The economic parallel is more than a convenient model for comparison. Corinne Low, a professor of Business Economics and Public Policy at the Wharton School, has gone so far as to chart women's reproductive capital on the US marriage market. 'Pricing the Biological Clock,' Low's 2016 paper, argues that the differential impact of aging on women's reproductive health negatively affects both a woman's relationship prospects and her future socio-economic outcomes. This, Low writes, 'is an inherent, biological asymmetry between men and women: whereas for men the reproductive system ages and declines in function at the same rate as other biological systems, for women this decline is much earlier and swifter than other aging processes.' Low finds evidence that this asymmetry has real economic consequences for women, impacting their willingness to invest in human capital, since such investments take time, and may therefore limit their appeal on the marriage market.

To prove this, Low sets up an experiment that assigns a randomly generated age to an online dating profile as a means of determining whether men's apparent preference for younger women has to do with aesthetic attraction or a valuation of her prospective fertility. From there, she collects information about participants' conscious age preferences for a hypothetical partner, their levels of education, incomes, and the dating profiles they wound up choosing. She finds that men have a strong preference for younger partners, even when beauty and other factors are controlled for, and that this preference is driven by men who have no children and have accurate knowledge of the age-fertility trade-off. Low concludes that each additional year of a woman's age means she would need to earn an additional $7,000 for her potential partner to be indifferent – the market price of her fertility, a rapidly depreciating economic asset.

The figures paint a clear picture. It is not only emotionally fraught and potentially crazy but quite literally economically disadvantageous for women to end relationships with men who meet the requirements to be deemed 'a catch.' While evaluating the market price of fertility is, to say the least, unromantic, partnership has always, on some level, functioned as a contract. Where it comes to marriage, that legislative component is literal: a formal, legal union of individuals and assets.

But what partnership and romantic love respectively entail have changed dramatically over a relatively short time. It's easy to forget that it wasn't so long ago that partnership and romantic love were seen as separate entities. In another, not-so-distant era, Taylor Swift would have sung about her future husband's goats.

2

The Birth of Love, and Liberty

I wasn't the type of young person to seek out Jane Austen on my own. Period manners and marriage plots? Thanks, but pass; I'd seen *Clueless* and was pretty sure I got the gist. But with few discernable interests apart from books (and tastes that, I'm mortified to report, leaned more toward Bukowski than Brontë), combined with an even less developed sense of professional aptitude, my undergrad self ended up settling into a new identity as an English lit major. Austen, naturally, became a part of my new life. My eighteenth-century British lit professor, an affable young adjunct with a clump of Day-Glo orange hair, put *Pride and Prejudice* squarely on the syllabus during our semester on the Romantic era. This novel, he told us, signalled a major shift in social values, and was therefore important to understand. Not exactly a ringing endorsement.

Pride and Prejudice famously concerns the courtship of a family of sisters who need to marry into money to preserve the family's social standing as members of the landed gentry. The new, period-specific catch is that the sisters should also, ideally, be fond of the well-off dudes they marry — and it's this new requirement of affability, even maybe something akin to love, that leads to dramatic tension and lessons learned by all. But to me, it barely seemed worthy of being called a predicament.

When I encountered Austen's Bennet sisters, I was nineteen, and newly into a relationship with someone who was prematurely wise, financially stable, and a clear marrying type — in other words, my exact opposite in at least three non-trivial areas. I felt utterly unequipped to parse the competing priorities of my romantic future, the balance of love and stability, companionship, and eroticism. It seemed much less intimidating to accept an eligible suitor on the simple grounds of mutual regard and material security – to say, 'I like your bank account and can tolerate your person,' and move on. The clear directive to simply secure an economically advantageous match would have certainly taken the guesswork out of my own romantic future. I'd been brought up with the same expectations of a majority of my straight-leaning female friends: that it was not just possible but preferable to expect *everything* from one person, forever.

Austen's era marked a relatively new way of thinking about the role of marriage, one organized on the individualistic notion of personal happiness rather than the participation in a tradition of social and family organization. The Romantic period made way, you could say, for *romance*. And in Austen's novels, the folly implicit in the pursuit of romance drives the action. Not that Austen was herself a fool for love; as a writer and thinker she acutely recognized that the ideal relationship is a tough one to come by. (It feels mean but important to mention here that Austen died alone.)

Even considering how she put love on the agenda, the expectations of marriage Austen laid out in her works, by the standards of their twenty-first-century analogs, verge on the enviably quaint. Contemporary relationship narratives apply unending pressure to settle *down* without ever settling *for*. We are told, loud and clear and over and over, that Mr. Right will come along, and he'll give us butterflies and the feeling of home, he'll be our best friend and the man of our dreams. To compromise would guarantee a lifetime of regret and undermine our self-respect – the opposite of the girl power we've grown up with.

Austen's heroines have been beloved through the ages because they still read as wise, rising above the bullshit that their more tragic foils inevitably succumb to. Elizabeth Bennet only accepts the hand of wealthy suitor Mr. Darcy once she recognizes his strength of character. Her younger sister Lydia, meanwhile, narrowly escapes social ruin by taking up with the moneyless cad Wickham, who then has to be bribed into marrying her. Austen's heroines do not compromise; they just happen to gravitate toward their most ideal outcome, as though self-interest were commensurate with moral fortitude.

Likewise, it's only by holding ourselves to the implausible-on-paper standards of mate selection that we might arrive at the end game of a forever-match equipped to tick off any remaining 'to-dos' from our self-actualization checklists. I grew up understanding that, for a smart and self-sufficient woman, a partner wasn't necessarily the be-all and end-all of life … except that it sort of, actually, was.

When considering coupledom as something that eventually leads to a lifelong commitment, we, understandably, weigh the pros and cons of a given relationship carefully. Do we aim for security or sustained chemistry, we might ask ourselves, or risk shooting for both at once (and then some)? Do we factor in our attachment to our partner's families or treat our significant other as an independent entity and our union as an island – or maybe a two-island archipelago in the variably navigable waters of life? (Do two islands even count as an archipelago? Are fixed landmasses an appropriate analogy for beings that move – maybe even apart – through time?) And, possibly, a scale-tipping question that pertained just as much to the Bennet sisters as it does to the average woman today: when men continue to hold significantly greater earning power than women, is it vulgar to consider economics?

A recent analysis by the American Association of University Women shows that women in the US bear approximately two-thirds of the nation's student-debt burden, borrowing more and more than our male classmates, only to earn less after graduation. These figures are comparable in Canada, according to data from the Government of Canada's Budget 2017 Gender Statement, and nearly identical in the UK as well. In truth, I simply would not have weathered the financial unpredictability of an early writing career if I hadn't met and loved a good man with a great job, one who shouldered the bulk of our shared bills. While a sizable number of my creative-aspirant peers quietly bridged sporadic paycheques with parental subsidies, my boyfriend and I shared a cheap apartment where the distribution of expenses was income-proportional, and the only strings attached were our shared and indefinite future.

My ambivalence over this state of financial affairs has continued to linger beyond the borders of that relationship. To be clear: we were in love. Yet, it's also true that during the years that I racked up the chops and bylines I hoped would eventually secure my financial independence, I felt like a kept woman. I wanted a relationship that was altruistic and fair, but I also wanted the experience of self-sufficiency. I hated feeling beholden. And I continue to reap what I hated.

We weren't technically married, but in Canada, where we lived, our common-law partnership was legally regarded as though we were. I didn't make the choice to be there simply because he made more money than I did, even if I benefited from it; on the contrary, I believe this dynamic contributed to the relationship's demise. Studies have found that financial harmony within a long-term partnership is essential for that partnership's success. And being partnered at all is considered essential for financial harmony, period. Even so, I'm not above speculating who has or hasn't 'married for money' with the judgmental undertones that imply I would only tie the knot for some other reason. But most of us, speaking frankly, *are* marrying for money. At least in part. The contract of marriage was founded as an economic alliance and it remains as much today: shared roof, shared bills, shared wealth or lack thereof. If it weren't, we wouldn't need to involve the state to make it real, nor lawyers to make it stop.

What has been par for the course throughout the history of courtship, and under scrutiny by Austen, remains true today. Somehow, still, it's a (white) man's world. Men of means in particular hold disproportionate power in the heterosexual quest for companionship, a cliché echoed on celebrity tabloid magazine covers and in romantic comedy plot lines, recurrent in a subclass of *New York Times* wedding announcement that may or may not make mention of a much younger bride's 'wisdom beyond her years.' My best friend and I sometimes joke about the distant-future day when our devoted male partners will decide to direct their gravity-yielding anatomy toward tenderer – yet improbably still willing – pastures. Neither of us believes this would actually happen to us, but there's a fatalism to our breezy texts.

Possibly for better than worse, ours is an era of techno-logically enhanced sexual transparency. Everyone's on

Tinder and OkCupid, Bumble and/or any other number of apps for managing the burden of finding love (be it for life or the afternoon). There are even nakedly transactional dating sites for married couples seeking an affair, and for facilitating 'sugar baby' configurations between (usually) young women and wealthy older men, though same-sex and sugar momma pairings are also brokered by such sites. The latter cohort are seeking an 'arrangement' – one of the aforementioned sites is literally called SeekingArrangement – that blurs the boundaries between sex work and plain old-fashioned dating, typically involving an exchange of material provisions for companionship and sex.

The trademarked slogan of SeekingArrangement is 'Mutually Beneficial Arrangements,' only barely euphemistic. The site's implied market exchange of young female sex and older male wealth replicates a cultural paradigm so familiar to the average North American adult that there's barely a need to elaborate on what exactly an 'arrangement' entails. (As it happens, the site operates across 139 countries worldwide.)

To either cover its tracks or assuage the moral hang-ups of its pricklier clientele, the website's language uses the words 'relationship' and 'arrangement' interchangeably. It's a clever bit of branding, given that while most people are able to suss out what's beneath the wink-and-nod, anyone who's ever been in a relationship will agree that all partnerships require some degree of compromise. The basis of every partnership is matching one's preferred give-and-takes with those of someone else. SeekingArrangement reasons that its site gives couples a leg (or something) up on coupledom by letting each party be upfront about at least a few major expectations off the bat. Aren't we all, in some way, seeking an arrangement?

There have been moments when I've found myself sheepishly jealous of what SeekingArrangement calls 'the Sugar Lifestyle,' a transactional approach to partnership that doesn't pretend to ignore the economic imbalance between parties, nor the dating-market commodity of youth. Not that it's in my constitution to feign approval at the type of man who believes he has 'earned' lots of money, but maybe life would have been easier in the medium term if I'd held my nose and plunged headfirst into the sugar bowl as a twenty-four-year-old. Even then, I was acutely aware of the specific time-sensitive desirability I held, as a woman just over the threshold of my twenties, and I also appreciated that I still held the cards to play that deck if I felt like it – an insurance policy whose finite nature no woman recognizes more than one who is only barely an adult.

But these days it seems unromantic, at best, to suggest that romance and pragmatism are diametrically opposed ideals, even if people's mating habits often tell a different story. Nearly one in five Americans will fess up to having cheated on their partners, despite a widely held understanding of infidelity as an ultimate act of betrayal. While I agree with pretty much everyone that partnering for romantic compatibility is ideal, I've also spent many agonizing hours interrogating the odds of my own ability to sustain romantic connectivity with the same human being over the course of a lifetime. It feels good to be devoted to a person you love and who loves you back, yes. But people grow, either in parallel, together, or apart, and emotional compasses don't hold fast to magnetic north.

Social values are the product of conditioning, informed by our own living conditions and what we've learned from those who came before us. And, where it comes to following your heart, 'those who came before us' is a relatively short list. Love hasn't always been conceptually tied up in the context of a singular forever-marriage. In fact, it wasn't until the eighteenth century that anyone really did the marrying-for-love thing at all. A majority of people, across the history of humanity, had agreed that the risk was simply too high.

The ancient Romans, for instance, viewed marriage as a necessary drudge for securing wealth, property, and the continuation of the (patriarchal) bloodline. Likewise, it didn't need to last forever. By the late Republic era, both men and women could divorce and remarry at will and, though technically illegal among women, adultery was common and even playfully encouraged. In his *Ars Amatoria* (*The Art of Love*), the poet Ovid instructs aspiring male side pieces to 'be courteous' to the husbands of their would-be female lovers. 'Nothing could better serve your plans than to be in his good graces,' he adds, in what reads something like a prim Latin prologue to *The Ethical Slut*.

Roman life was hard, and the consensus seems to have been that marriage was too serious an endeavour to be muddled by the irrational demands of the heart. I'm not kidding: a Republican Roman senator named Manlius was booted from the Senate for kissing his wife in front of their own daughter. Maybe Stoicism was to blame for the distrust of capital-F Feelings with regard to sex and marriage (and sex *in* marriage), and it was a line of thinking that trickled into early Christian thought – and, arguably, continues to be echoed in the family-values rhetoric of some religious conservatives.

Stoic teachings like the philosopher Seneca the Younger's apprehension that 'there is nothing more disgusting than making love to your wife as if she were your mistress' found parallels in early Christian writings on the subject of sex. The Apostle Paul, arguably the chief architect of the Church, was in fact a contemporary of Seneca the Younger. There still exists a series of back-and-forth letters attributed to the pair, and while this correspondence has been broadly dismissed as apocryphal, there are clear similarities in the two figures' lines of thinking. In his letters to the Galatians, Paul issued an anti-lust warning that framed sexual desire as, if not all-out gross, definitely a hindrance to one's spiritual purpose: 'Walk by the Spirit, and do not gratify the desires of the flesh. For the desires of the flesh are against the Spirit, and the desires of the Spirit are against the flesh; for these are opposed to each other, to prevent you from doing what you would.'

Only later, in the seventh chapter of Paul's First Epistle to the Corinthians, he tweaks his directive. People should absolutely gratify their fleshly desires, he allows, so long as the act takes place within the confines of marriage. Yet, one hardly gets the impression that Paul had undergone some sex-positive change of heart. On the contrary, he implies that self-denial tempts more lust than a person might be able keep a lid on, which would make the suffering party susceptible to extramarital fornication: 'Do not deprive one another, except perhaps by agreement for a limited time, that you may devote yourselves to prayer; but then come together again, so that Satan may not tempt you because of your lack of self-control.' Paul basically prescribes non-procreative marital sex as a type of carnal harm reduction, and it's safe to presume that he was less than overjoyed about this provision.

Over three centuries later, Saint Augustine (who brought to his sex-cautious writings the wisdom of exhaustive firsthand knowledge, detailed in his *Confessions*) would be the first to confer sacramental status onto marriage. The North African bishop wrote two of the foundational texts of early Christian theology and undertook a rigorous study of the Old and New Testaments in order to arrive at a theological framework for the early Church's position on corporeal desire. He decreed that sex within marriage was inevitable, if not ideal; outside of marriage, a definite no. Marriage was recast as a permanent union, and divorce a venial sin.

Augustine's influential ascetic streak was reinforced by the writings of his comparably rigid contemporary, Saint Jerome, who viewed sex that was not conducted for the explicit purposes of procreation (even in marriage) as a mortal sin. These early Christian moral constraints on desire, which maintained an idealized incarnation of sexuality that kept itself contained in the proverbial pants, further reinforced the idea of marriage as specifically a conjugal union between two people.

Courtship, the historical precursor to the concept of the love marriage, was also a by-product of the Christian Church, if indirectly. Some academics attribute the medieval trope of courtly love, which emerged in the twelfth century, to changes in Church doctrine that emphasized both a woman's consent in her own marriage and, alongside that, a more spiritual relationship to God that emphasized personal connection and emotional attachment. This shift coincided with the Crusades, during which the literary tradition of courtly love sprung forth. These were typically stories about romances between married noblewomen, whose husbands may or may not be off fighting religious wars, and amorous knights. Courtly romances extolled chivalrous ritual in place of overt libido, the High Middle Ages' version of breathless high school affairs.

As the spread of Christianity bumped against the whims of aristocrats and kings, both men and (more discreetly) women had continued conducting their own private romances outside the confines of marriage. But the cult of courtly love elevated these extramarital pursuits beyond the carnal and into the spiritual realm. The romances these stories sketched were intense and fleeting, consumed by an audience of bored noblewomen – one-handed reads for the medieval set.

Sometimes the authors of courtly romances were in direct patronage of their intended audience. Both Chrétien de Troyes and Andreas Capellanus, who authored *The Art of Courtly Love*, were beneficiaries of Marie of France, Countess of Champagne. The countess was herself the daughter of a renowned muse of courtly love, Norman queen Eleanor of Aquitaine, whose legend includes tell of a likely consummated romance with a renowned troubadour. In Marie's narrative role as courtly love rule-maker in Capellanus's etiquette guide, the (married) countess explicitly warns that it is impossible for love to 'exert its powers between two people who are married to each other.'

The cult of courtly love was probably more of a fictional trope than an insight into the sex lives of medieval nobles. Neverthelesss, it offered a template for the union of ritualized romantic pursuit and emotional drama that would re-enter the fore during the time of Austen – this time, in the context of marriage. In the interim, the average European marriage probably had little in common with any courtly romance. Historian Stephanie Coontz, in her book *Marriage, a History: How Love Conquered Marriage*, drops this sixteenth-century

English rhyming proverb: 'A spaniel, a woman, and a walnut tree, the more they're beaten the better they be.' If this startling suggestion of spousal relations reads as a precursor to the misogyny of contemporary men's-rights discussion boards online, that's probably because it is. (Also, please don't hit your pups.)

But a change was in motion, albeit slowly. Beginning in the fourteenth century, a revived pan-European interest in classical philosophy and literature emerged to challenge the no-fun chokehold of the Roman Catholic Church. Gutenberg's invention of the printing press, a century later, only hastened the process, and, with the concurrent Protestant Reformation, a newly splintered Western Church decentralized religious control.

Meanwhile, advances in science fuelled a proliferation of information that supplanted religious doctrine with reason, a humanistic movement that culminated with the eighteenth-century Age of Enlightenment. A cultural secularization that touted the pursuit of individual rights and happiness became easier to actualize with the advent of industry and the spread of a market economy. Some scholars, including Coontz, believe that the combined cultural and economic forces of the eighteenth century – the age of Austen – normalized the ideal of marrying for love. Industrialization gave rise to a new class of people whose access to wealth wasn't limited to agrarian land inheritance. As Friedrich Engels put it in his 1884 treatise *The Origin of the Family, Private Property and the State*, 'The creation of these "free" and "equal" people was precisely one of the main functions of capitalistic production.'

Industrialized economies also pulled people out of their kinship communities and into urban centres – a socially alienating experience that perhaps demanded the intimate salve of so-called romantic love. Cambridge University professor emeritus Alan Macfarlane writes in *The Culture of Capitalism*: 'Depending on how one regards the "romantic love complex," it could be seen as one of the compensations for the loneliness and isolation of a disintegrated, associational, society, or as yet another curse produced by the disintegration of the old community bonds.' The economic makings of his so-called 'romantic love complex' break down simply enough:

> Markets opened up, mobility increased, people were caught up in a new and open environment with money and market values dominant. Secondly, capitalism improved the standard of living. This altered the material conditions of life. Thirdly, capitalism, or more particularly its manifestation in a particular industrial form, led to the break up of the rural communities. People were sucked into an urban and industrial proletariat.

This new urban and industrial proletariat eroded the reliance on extended familial networks and political allegiances that had, throughout history, ensured economic survival. In its place sprouted the individual, left to their own devices. And so began the emergence of some idea that the love-marriage was, if not precisely a human right, then at least a definite possibility. Suddenly, there was the impetus to make partnership decisions that satisfied a spectrum of needs that had previously been met by more than one person or, more likely, sublimated in service of family, the Church, and the gruelling demands of agrarian life.

In Colonial New England, a similar change was taking place. The period's conduct books (predecessors to the self-help book) give a comparatively hard-edged insight into the changing attitudes surrounding courtship and domesticity in the eighteenth and nineteenth centuries. In *Letters to a Young Lady*, an etiquette manual whose first edition dates to 1791 (twenty-two years prior to *Pride and Prejudice*), the Reverend John Bennett dispenses criteria for optimal partnering that wouldn't be out of place in a contemporary self-help manual. (Then, as now, these books were written to impart upon readers the etiquette of the age, while also offering advice for making productive – and pragmatic – choices.)

A Connecticut preacher, Bennett gently puts forward that a woman should absolutely consider the realities of economics when choosing a husband. But his view of spousal selection factors a prospective spouse's displayed decorum *in addition to* financial stability, and places greater emphasis on the former. With decency of character, he argues, comes contentment – a view that's not altogether shocking from a Yankee Protestant man of the cloth. Even so, Bennett acknowledges that 'fortune surely should be considered' in the husband hunt, and especially when weighed against any romantic attachment that might or might not endure: 'It [would be] absurd to think of love, where there is not some prospect of a decent provision for your probable descendants.' But he also advises eligible ladies to knock down their expectations of what exactly constitutes 'decent provision' if the gentleman in question proves to be a decent human – suggesting, implicitly, that women should not consider prospective husbands as untapped wells of personal fortune and also, perhaps, that decent men are not a free-flowing commodity. 'Virtue and affection have an amazing power of inspiring contentment,' he writes. In other words, ladies, seek out a reliable provider who treats you with whatever qualifies as respect in your given social context, and upon whose sterling reputation you might build your own. It'll be fine!

This pragmatic, companionate view was not confined to the fledgling United States. Published in London, Mrs. Elizabeth Lanfear's 1824 *Letters to Young Ladies on Their Entrance into the World* takes the 'good man' directive a step further. In her view, 'affection may … be found a necessary ingredient with which to sweeten the cup of domestic care,' but feelings should be considered nice-to-haves and not necessities when separating the Husband Material from the chaff. Rather, 'the first and the most important considerations which should be attended to by a woman, before she forms a serious and irrevocable engagement, are the personal character, moral qualities, and mental endowments of the man who is to be her fellow-traveller in the great journey of life.' The image of marriage as a shared, companionate trek through earthly existence is gently egalitarian, but not exactly aligned with a heady pursuit of romance – nor reflective of the legal reality that a married woman was essentially an extension of her husband. So where, then, does good old-fashioned eros fit into this marital configuration?

Because the copyright laws of the eighteenth century weren't quite what they are today, entire phrases or chapters from one conduct manual might also appear, word for word, in dozens of others. This meant that one person's interpretation of a moment's social norms could be reproduced and repositioned as common wisdom time after time, over a span of decades. One warning dispelled verbatim in a handful of both men's and women's conduct manuals from the 1830s to the 1850s (and even an 1832 volume of the *Phrenological Journal*) echoes what we can assume, from its prolific and prolonged replication, was a popularly held view of women's character that we have yet to fully shake:

> Most women are inclined to be romantic. This tendency is not confined to the young or to the beautiful; to the intellectual, or to the refined. Romance is, indeed, the charm of female character … [But it] is associated in the minds of many with folly alone.

There's a lot to unpack in this ostensibly well-meaning passage, which was reproduced for mixed-gender audiences and with both male and female author credits. On the surface, it assumes that women are biologically wired to feel 'in love' more intensely than their male counterparts. But it also pathologizes this presumed imbalance between the genders as 'folly' – a deficit in judgment and, perhaps, in character. Women's silly little feelings are partly why they're so darn irresistible to the opposite sex; they are also, ultimately, why a woman's capacity for reason is inferior and, as such, requires that we be repeatedly reminded of what's best for them. For us.

Pronouncements that effectively align women's so-called inborn traits with their own oppression might feel retrograde, but versions of this rationale continue to be recycled into contemporary discussion, sometimes even under a guise of women's empowerment. It's not a massive leap from the gendered character dismissals of 1830s conduct manuals to, for instance, one bestselling self-help tome from the mid-2010s whose driving hypothesis was that women's continued workplace inequality sprung partly from a naturalized failure to self-advocate or, in the parlance of the author, to 'lean in.' One might observe that it's hardly a leap at all.

The passage also affirms a view of romantic tendency that has barely evolved in the two centuries since its first printing. We still tend to associate women with hearts that demand wooing, and men with a clumsy approach to getting the job done. A hugely influential (if also widely mocked) 1992 pop-psychology bestseller by John Gray went on to sell over 50 million copies under a gender-essentialist premise that purported that heterosexual women subconsciously continue to ascribe to the courtly love conventions of a damsel in distress waiting for her knight in shining armour to just rescue her, already. I will admit that I live in a cosmopolitan, careerist bubble. That said, I can't think of a single one of my millennial contemporaries who would seriously cite *Men Are from Mars, Women Are from Venus* as a work that contributed to their understanding of romantic relationships. Yet, the casual clickbait churn that occupies our social-media zone-outs often draws on similarly simple black-and-white dichotomies about identity and human relationships. Articles like '9 Things Guys Think Are Romantic, but Aren't' (in *Cosmo*) and 'This Is Why Guys Should Stop Giving "I F**ked Up" Flowers' (on Buzzfeed) litter the internet, suggesting that men are disinclined to receive women's emotional memos.

And, despite the British boy bands and Dominican bachata stars whose first-person testaments to tender masculinity endearingly stack twenty-first-century playlists, popular wisdom enforces a stereotype of emotionally integrated, heart-eyed women waiting for men to eventually either 'get it' or not. So widespread are these simplistic gendered notions of emotional incompatibility that I've often found myself – a self-diagnosed unromantic – assigning a dismissal of 'ugh, typical men' to moments where male paramours have failed to meet my emotional expectations. It's a thing I've intermittently allowed myself to believe, in a caveat-studded way, despite my resistance to universal truths.

But intermittent incantations to 'end all men' aren't driven by a belief that men are simply not wired to comprehend, let alone meet, my emotional needs. Rather, I've internalized at least some version of the view that men and women tend to be socialized to develop different skill sets, and that women get the ones that make them less infuriating. You could even say that the expectation has become a self-fulfilling prophecy.

In real life, the scope of humanity is vast and multifaceted. The notion of gender itself as an intrinsically hardwired, anatomical either-or is being progressively dismantled by social theorists and a growing populace of nuanced thinkers who've lost patience with the status quo. It's a measure of progress that, as society relies increasingly less on adhering to emotional and economic labour roles defined by gender, individuals can opt out of that system of classification altogether. For now, the decision to do so takes on an identity charged with political implication and social repercussions, threats of ostracism and violence. But one day, it likely won't. To (yes, unironically, though with all applicable caveats in place) borrow from John Grey's 2017 follow-up to his initial foray into Venus and Mars, couples today expect to be soulmates rather than gendered 'role mates.' The conscious expectation for equal emotional fulfillment has come to absolutely supplant the previously prescribed heterosexual desire for a male breadwinner counterpart to the caregiving matriarch. The germ for just such a dynamic was planted in the Enlightenment and nurtured to fruition in its Industrial aftermath.

As a market-based economy enriched an expanded bourgeoisie throughout Europe and the Americas, growing numbers of men and women were given access to a pageantry of courtship that had previously been confined to the aristocracy. Women 'came out' into society and were pursued by male suitors, whom they were then able to either accept or reject in an artificially inflated rite of agency.

Whether we've escaped the woman-as-object/man-as-actor dichotomy is a matter of perspective. Yet, it's hard to believe that within such a short period, we were given the basis for a romantic ideal that has grown to shape a multi-billion-dollar dating industry, an even more profitable wedding-industrial complex, and the barely tenable fairy tale that keeps the two afloat: that every woman can be the author of her own happy ending. But with autonomy comes great responsibility to either choose exactly right or to undermine the very existence of our own freedom to follow our hearts.

Viewed through this historical lens, the works of Jane Austen are all the more poignant. That they concern the specific matters of marriage and love at a moment in time where both concepts were shifting is why they remain so satisfying, and even relatable, two centuries later. Marrying for love in addition to security was not yet something to be taken for granted; it was loaded, and it was stressful. *Pride and Prejudice* in particular imbues its depiction of the mechanics of spousal selection with what I think is a rare, appropriate amount of ambivalence.

The novel also gives an over-the-top worst-case scenario in the Bennet parents' unhappy marriage. Mr. and Mrs. Bennet's cartoonishly wretched match reads as a peripheral plot motif on the novel's surface, but its cautionary message drives the internal conflict of the Bennet daughters' own respective quests to pin down a mate. Mr. Bennet is beneath Mrs. Bennet's financial station; Mrs. Bennet is, in turn, completely daft. Equal footing never stood a chance. The bookish (but economically sub-optimal) Mr. Bennet married his beautiful, airheaded wife on a youthful whim and has spent the intervening decades in sullen regret, alternately brooding in his study and making belittling cracks at his wife and daughters. But he has a soft spot for the shrewd Elizabeth, and warns her to avoid repeating his mistake: 'Unless you truly esteemed your husband ... [y]our lively talents would place you in the greatest danger in an unequal marriage. You could scarcely escape discredit and misery.'

Austen doesn't exactly beat around the bush in making sure readers recognize that the elder Bennets were an ill-suited match from the start, with their incompatible temperaments and asymmetrical bank balances. The consequences of such a careless union, she proposes, are far from whimsical. By marrying beneath her financial station, Mrs. Bennet has shortchanged her daughters' future prospects. But the real emphasis here is on Mr. Bennet, bitter and withdrawn after two decades of marriage to someone he doesn't particularly respect or enjoy being around; Mrs. Bennet, in turn, has no choice but to endure the sarcastic barbs of a husband who can't stand her, and whom she doesn't understand. It's hell for both parties, and a cautionary tale for Austen's readers.

The Bennet parents' marriage might be one of the most loudly flapping red flags of modern literary history. Both husband and wife are paying a price for an impulsive union built upon a superficial mutual attraction and, boy, the result is sub-ideal. Mr. Bennet's advice to Elizabeth against an 'unequal marriage' serves as a literary *aha* moment, and becomes our protagonist's guiding star. Discredit and misery: hardly ideal planes of existence, and incidentally also the precise flavours of doom that careless women can expect from marrying someone they don't respect.

Austen's works are a gleaming full-length mirror of the society that informed them. As with most revolutionary social developments, the transition from an ideal marriage of pure pragmatism to one of romantic companionship wasn't immediate. Fledgling understandings of romantic autonomy did little to calm people's anxieties around choosing the wrong spouse; if anything, the birth of love-marriage elevated the sense of stakes involved in mate selection. Austen's Regency heroines belonged to a landed gentry that relied on well-chosen marriages to preserve class respectability and protect individual families' wealth, but, further to that, there was no legal recourse – short of provable catastrophe – for a man or woman who felt they'd made the wrong choice.

3

Lie Back and Think of Paperwork

The fate of a union has always been determined by its particular circumstance. Romantic ideals are a point of privilege and access, and not all post-Enlightenment women have been entitled to the careful consideration of potential mates. As the real-life counterparts to Austen's nineteenth-century heroines were contemplating pragmatism and love in marriage, for example, enslaved Black people in the southern United States were forbidden legal marriage at all. An estimated two out of every five informal slave marriages were broken up when one spouse was sold off to another plantation; entire generations of families were torn apart, reconstituted, and broken again. Even when accounting for the concentration of Anglo-American and British case studies I've referenced, it's critical to recognize the roles race and class each play in the basic existential freedoms of choice in all areas of life.

Every partnership must contend with the issue of logistics. Even among the more privileged denizens of the West at the turn of the nineteenth century, not everyone lived in a community that included a justice of the peace or a law clerk. Among rural white settlers in eighteenth- and nineteenth-century United States, common-law marriages were not uncommon workarounds for a lack of clerical or financial access to proper ceremonial pomp. In the UK, the Marriage Act of 1753 prohibited couples from pursuing clandestine marriages that skirted the fees required for legal marriage licences, which prompted many poorer Britons to follow suit in opting for unmarried cohabitation. And across social strata, women had fewer fundamental rights than were generally afforded men, and even these were typically further eroded when they became wives.

Theoretically, unmarried white women in the Anglo world could, ironically, enjoy freedoms of property ownership throughout the eighteenth and nineteenth centuries. This holdout of 'coverture,' a thirteenth-century English common law, recognized single adult women as sole legal entities, but only until they were wed. Upon marriage, they forfeited their lawful personhood and became, in the eyes of Church and law, an extension of their husbands' persons. Under *cover*ture, a woman's rights were literally *covered* by those of her husband. While it's tempting to describe historical marriage as husband's de facto ownership of wife, it might be more accurate to call it erasure. It is a perhaps unpleasant truth that the continued practice of women taking their husband's surnames upon marriage can also trace its origins to coverture, a symbolic remnant of dark-age convention we've yet to collectively shake.

Coverture was observed in both the 'old' world and the new. In the continental United States of the eighteenth and nineteenth centuries, a married woman might be entitled to own property depending on where she lived and the circumstances of her husband. As early as 1771, women in the then-Province of Pennsylvania were allowed to own property in their own names, but only if their spouses were somehow unable to manage it themselves. The later Married Women's Property Act, passed in New York in 1848, established that a single woman's property could remain lawfully hers even after marriage, and that she could also obtain her own earnings and gifts as a wife. Over the following decade, a majority of states would pass similar statutes.

Upper Canada (what is now Ontario) established a property rights act for married women in 1859, beating the UK by eleven years. When Britain finally did pass its Married Women's Property Act in 1870, critics worried that the stride toward a more equal treatment of men and women – even if limited to the sole regard of property entitlement – would wreak havoc within marriages. In fact, it wasn't until the Married Women's Property Act of 1882 that the former act would be revised to recognize English husbands and wives as independent legal entities.

It's easy to understand why women of limited means would have chosen to marry, given few alternate avenues for livelihood. But why would a woman of a property-owning class opt to surrender her independence in exchange for a husband? One major impetus was the social cost of spinsterhood, whose stigmatization grew in direct correlation with the post-Enlightenment glorification of marriage. Stephanie Coontz writes that the word *spinster* was 'originally an honorable term reserved for a woman who spun yarn, [which] by the 1600s ... had come to mean any woman who was not married.' A century later, the word took on connotation closer to the negative one it presently has. '[T]he flip side,' Coontz explains, 'of the new reverence accorded to wives.'

And that reverence was real. With the emergence of a companionate, affectionate marriage ideal came increased social pressure for women to endeavour upon the project of cheerful domesticity. Marriage and the family became recoded as arenas for women's spiritual actualization, the locus for pure fulfillment as opposed to a plane of existence largely grounded in duty. In a sense, post-Enlightenment wifehood took on the set of signifiers we still see reinforced by a certain style of mommy blog and lifestyle Instagram account in the twenty-first century. Here, a life initiated in an unanaesthetized home birth becomes told for a consuming public through a series of photogenic vignettes that establish a simulacra of maternal serenity.

The likeliest reason for free, propertied women's persistence in marrying is also the least surprising: throughout history, women had been brought up to believe that their primary destiny in secular life was to become a wife and mother. A woman's selfhood had always been defined in relation to others. In the absence of a husband, what might her existence even mean?

And besides, there was also the matter of sex. The moral indignation reserved for unmarried women caught in a man's carnal snares was ruinous, especially if the indiscretion produced a child. Many of these women wound up in asylums or labour homes under the guise of religious charity, effectively plucked from society and stained for life. Just a year before scandalously having her own child out of wedlock, Mary Wollstonecraft lambasted the attitudes of the era in *A Vindication of the Rights of Women* (1792). 'Still, highly as I respect marriage, as the foundation of almost every social virtue, I cannot avoid feeling the most lively compassion for those unfortunate females who are broken off from society, and by one error torn from all those affections and relationships that improve the heart and mind,' Wollstonecraft wrote. She thought this unfair; a young woman caught off guard by a man's advances might genuinely believe herself to be in love.

Though spared the so-called charity reserved for a 'ruined' woman, a miserably married woman's fate was hardly any better. Until the mid-nineteenth century, divorce was unheard of among ordinary people, and women were expected to endure adultery, emotional mistreatment, and even some measure of physical abuse as part of the contract of marital obedience.

In the UK, the Matrimonial Causes Act of 1857 finally institutionalized the country's first court tasked with hearing divorce cases in the event of, as its title stated, a cause worthy of dissolution. But it was much easier for men to obtain divorces than it was for women. The Act entitled men to file for divorce solely on the grounds of a wife's adultery; women, on the other hand, had to prove that their husbands had committed adultery *in addition to* bigamy, incest, cruelty, or desertion. The Canadian historian Elizabeth Abbott writes that the effect of the new UK law was a fifty-fold increase in divorce. Yet some 600,000 women petitioned Queen Victoria against it, objecting both to the gendered double standard it perpetuated and to its violation of the 'indissoluble marriage to which we have adhered since England was England.' Wanting an unbreakable marriage was undoubtedly driven in large part by the culture's sanctification of the institution, but a woman's inability to inherit her own property – or keep any of her husband's, in the event of a divorce – certainly didn't hurt in fostering the desire to remove any lingering trace of a simple marital exit.

In the US, few states recognized cruelty as grounds for a divorce prior to 1840. Even then, what constituted marital cruelty was open to legal interpretation. American historian Robert L. Griswold writes that 'cruelty' as grounds for divorce was generally understood to encompass either physical violence or the threat thereof, but records show

scholar Joyce W. Warren. Many believed that adopting the issue as a cause would present as anti-family and hinder the suffrage movement; others were put off by the secularization of marriage, which would reposition spousehood as just a contract, as opposed to a sacramental bond.

Elizabeth Cady Stanton's 1884 article 'The Need of Liberal Divorce Laws' was likely intended to win over her fellow feminists as much as the general public. 'Divorce is not the foe of marriage,' wrote Stanton. 'Adultery, intemperance, licentiousness are its foes. One might as well speak of medicine as the foe of health.' Stanton had a point, and others were catching on. Despite the social and economic impetus to remain unhappily married, rates of divorce rose exponentially from the middle of the nineteenth century into the second decade of the twentieth – a legally upheld expression of individual agency, afforded those who the courts saw as people. Then and now, the freedom to make relationship decisions was not a privilege within all women's grasp.

4
A Love Freely Chosen

I first encountered the 1857 Dred Scott decision in a high school textbook as a blip in a chapter about a series of events that precipitated the United States Civil War. I'd learned that Scott was a slave who had lived with his master in the free state of Illinois and the free territory of Wisconsin and who, upon return to the slaveholding state of Missouri, had unsuccessfully appealed to the Supreme Court for his freedom. I had no idea that the landmark case hinged on whether Scott's civilly recognized marriage conferred upon him other inalienable legal rights as a person.

As I'd been taught it, Scott's prior residence in places where slavery was illegal had been lain out in court as grounds for his emancipation. When Chief Justice Roger Taney wrote out his ruling against Scott's freedom, it was on the premise that blacks had 'no rights which the white man is bound to respect.' With Scott held up as an example, Taney declared that, yes, a slave could absolutely be taken into non-slaveholding territories and, no, a Black American could never be considered a free US citizen. As I learned in high school, the Dred Scott decision is now broadly recognized as one of the chief catalysts for the American Civil War, and it is retold today primarily from that perspective. But it is also equally a story of the legal implications of family-making for Black people in the US during and after slavery, specifically with regard to marriage, if seldom presented as one.

Sometime in 1837, or possibly 1838, in Fort Snelling, Wisconsin Territory, the marriage of Harriet Robinson and Dred Scott was presided over by US Army Major Lawrence

Taliaferro. As an Indian agent assigned to the fortification, Taliaferro mediated relations between American Fur Company traders and the Ojibwa and Dakota peoples who lived in and around the settlement, brokering treaties to further US government interests in westward expansion. Taliaferro served as Justice of the Peace within the outpost and, as a member of the Presbyterian Church in an area without a designated priest or chaplain, oversaw the Robinson-Scott wedding vested in the powers of both Church and state.

Harriet Robinson was Taliaferro's slave, despite living north of the Mason-Dixon line in a territory where slavery was not technically legal. Though the purchase and sale of slave chattel was prohibited outside of the designated slave-holding southern states by 1804, the Army tolerated slavery in and around its fortifications, including those in the north.

Scott was enslaved by the army surgeon Dr. John Emerson, who assumed ownership of both Dred and Harriet after the wedding. Emerson's army duties required that he switch posts frequently, and it wasn't long after the ceremony that the doctor would be called to relocate to the Jefferson Barracks Military Post near St. Louis, at which point he left the Scotts behind to live something resembling a free life as a family. It would be short-lived.

In early 1838, during his travels, Emerson met and married Eliza (Irene) Sanford at Fort Jesup in Louisiana, and sent for Dred and Harriet to join them. Over the next two years the Emersons, with the growing Scott family in tow, would bounce from Fort Jesup back up to Fort Snelling, then to St. Louis.

Then in 1842, Dr. and Mrs. Emerson left St. Louis for Florida, where John was to fight in the Second Seminole

War – more accurately, a guerrilla rebellion on the part of Seminoles in Florida, and a number of Black allies, in the face of US government efforts to push them west. It's likely the Emersons left Dred, Harriet, and their two young daughters behind in Missouri; slaveholders were discouraged from bringing their slaves to the Florida front, out of a widely held concern that slaves would be sympathetic to the Seminole resistance. During this time, in the absence of their slaveholders, the Scotts would again have lived a family life that hinted at freedom.

Four years later, emboldened by the abolitionist preacher at Harriet Scott's church, Dred and Harriet each individually filed suits against their mistress, Irene Emerson, in the St. Louis County Circuit Court, to petition for their freedom. Their legal case hinged on the argument that a state-sanctioned marriage, performed in a territory that did not recognize slavery, conferred free status upon both parties that could not be revoked. Their suits merged and made it to the US Supreme Court, which, in 1857, ruled against the Scotts in a decision that sent shockwaves across the Union.

Legal scholars have since considered whether the case would have ended differently if Harriet, and not Dred, had been the plaintiff. Harriet had lived in free territory for longer, a free person in the eyes of the law even if that was not reflected in the reality of her situation. In a fascinating (and retrospectively heartbreaking) 1997 case study for the *Yale Journal of Law*, authors Lea VanderVelde and Sandhya Subramanian propose that Harriet had the stronger case; in 'giving' Harriet to marriage and presiding over its attendant civil ceremony as Justice of the Peace, Major Taliaferro was granting Harriet her freedom. By extension, as her legally recognized husband, Dred would be free as well. A legally married slave was effectively a contradiction in terms.

For both free and enslaved Blacks in the American Antebellum period, the systemic suppression of both basic humanity and free will rendered the bond of partnership precarious at best. In law and in practice, freedom was a transient state that a Black person living either in or outside of the South might enter and leave throughout the course of their life. One generation of free people did not guarantee the next. And yet, despite the constant threat of separation and intergenerational upheaval, marriage was observed among slaves and free Blacks alike. Or, at least, a version of marriage.

By and large, the law didn't recognize marriage between slaves, because the law didn't recognize slaves as people. But over the course of the Antebellum period, some jurisdictions adopted stances on slave marriage that could be construed (and, at the time, likely were) as marginally less inhumane than the status quo. An 1819 Louisiana ruling granted slaves the right to so-called 'moral marriage' upon a master's consent, which would become a fully recognized civil marriage in the event of emancipation. The State of Tennessee similarly acknowledged de facto slave marriages, which could be created and ended at the whim of the couple's master or masters – an amendment that state lawmakers felt would 'ameliorate the condition of the slave.' But such case-specific provisions didn't change the fact that enslaved southerners of African descent were chattel, devoid of civil rights and the basic certainties enjoyed by free people. And besides, enslaved Blacks didn't own property that marriage would protect; rather, the logic went, they *were* property, so why bother?

But despite what was and wasn't legal, many slave owners allowed – and even encouraged – informal slave marriages. Likely unsurprising to modern readers, slave owners' permissiveness was influenced less by altruism than sheer economic self-interest. Enslaved husbands took care to help provide for their wives and families by whatever means available, whether hunting, fishing, or selling handmade goods. Wives, in turn, helped to mend and maintain the family's clothing and perhaps tend gardens for supplemental produce. The increased interdependency that slave marriage facilitated eased, for slave owners, the material burden of feeding and clothing their captive workforce.

Marriage also fit neatly into slaveholders' efforts to Christianize their slaves, a trend that echoes so many historical narratives of domination and conquest. As with the centuries of Western European colonizers (and their descendants) who have turned to religion as a means of rationalizing brutality and theft against Indigenous peoples' land, property, and lives, southern men of the cloth torqued scripture to defend the institution of slavery.

In 1850, the Baptist minister Thornton Stringfellow reasoned that slavery had bestowed upon millions of Blacks 'the range of Gospel influence,' without which they would have otherwise 'sunk down to eternal ruin.' Slavery, according to this reasoning, was actually a gift of eternal salvation disguised as barbarism. By encouraging informal Christian marriage between slaves, slaveholders reaped the incidental benefit of maintaining control over slaves' reproductive lives, ultimately multiplying their captive workforce. Slaves, meanwhile, didn't necessarily have a choice in who they would end up marrying.

Likewise, slaveholders had the power to separate families at will – and, all too frequently, they exercised it. Henry 'Box' Brown, who gained his nickname (and his freedom) by mailing himself from Richmond, Virginia, to Philadelphia in 1849, would later write: '[N]o slave husband has any certainty whatever of being able to retain his wife a single hour; neither has any wife any more certainty of her husband; their fondest affection may be utterly disregarded, and their devoted attachment cruelly ignored at any moment a brutal slave-holder may think fit.'

In the absence of personal liberty, Christian marriage – even if not legally upheld – may have provided some loose semblance of social capital within the confines of white, slave-owning society. As historian Tera W. Hunter writes, 'Membership in the Christian church affirmed community recognition of their bonds, provided a forum for airing and resolving disputes, and could potentially lead masters to think twice about spousal separations that were neither honorable nor obedient to the Christian spirit.'

Of course, the sheer existence of a slave economy makes clear that, legally and in practice, monetary self-interest had a nagging tendency to trump considerations of 'the Christian spirit' among the many who benefited from the material fruits of forced labour. Nonetheless, abolitionists appealed to the God-fearing sensibilities of slaveholding society by citing the callous separation of slave families as a damning strike against the institution. In an oft-cited 1858 address to the American Abolition Society, the Presbyterian minister George B. Cheever bellowed that 'for those most miserable outcasts of humanity, the American slaves,' the 'divine injunction' that husbands love their wives had been perverted, by slave owners, in the name of profit. '[Slave husbands] are not permitted to love,' said Cheever, 'but only in subjection to the price of the market, the necessities of [their] master, and the grand rule of [their] domestic institution, the slave and its increase.'

Ultimately, Cheever was right: whether or not everyone at the time could recognize the inherent inhumanity of slavery as an institution, slaveholders' concretely un-Christian treatment of slave families was tough to refute. In turn, Hunter writes that the Church contorted itself to reconcile the biblical hypocrisies that riddled its pro-slavery position. Certain Church concessions around slave marriage flew in the face of both civil and scriptural law, ironically affording slaves an unusual degree of leniency in some aspects of formal partnership. For instance, divorce was theoretically easier to obtain by slave couples than by free members of society (though it's worth repeating that such marriages were never civilly affirmed in the first place); the same is true of remarriage. That these minor potential freedoms were a function of the overall lack of control slaves had over their own family lives rendered their execution, as expressions of individual human will, effectively moot in the eyes of the lawmakers.

The records suggest that divorce was not a significant part of the family experience of slaves. Family separation resulting from the purchase and exchange of slaves, however, was. An estimated one-third of marriages between slaves born in slave-selling states were ripped apart by the interstate slave trade, which also separated one out of five enslaved children from one or both parents. Some one million more slaves were hired out on long-term contracts, swapped, or redistributed within slave-owning families onto different plantations.

It was common in the wake of a slaveholder's death for slaves to be divided among heirs; in the event of a wedding, slaves might be given as gifts. It was up to white slaveholding families to determine who would stay and who would go. In his lifetime, Henry 'Box' Brown would experience both forms of forced separation. By age fifteen, Brown's own brothers and sisters would be counted among the assets scattered away from the plantation they all had lived on, as a family, upon their master's death. Later, Brown would see his wife and three children taken to the auction block, purchased, and sent away – he has left a record of his memory of walking alongside the cart that carried them to their uncertain destination, holding, for several miles, the hand of his wife.

'[B]oth our hearts were so overpowered with feeling that we could say nothing,' Brown later wrote, 'and when at last we were obliged to part, the look of mutual love which we exchange was all the token which we could give each other that we should yet meet in heaven.'

When Brown made the choice to build a family, he knew what he was likely getting himself into. He married anyway, pledging to do anything in his power to keep his brood together. He obtained his (purportedly Christian) master's blessing before marrying his wife, Nancy, and she the same of hers; later, when Nancy and their children had been sold to a different master, Brown negotiated a payment plan to purchase his family's freedom. In a callous act of betrayal, it was the same master who had collected Brown's incremental payments who turned around and sold the family off. Brown, despondent, plotted his escape from bondage – a final desperate grasp toward some semblance of human agency.

Agency was what propelled slave families forward. In spite of the persistent existential threat faced by slave couples, a majority of slave marriages survived both the whims of the couple's masters and of each partner's own hearts. Within the confines of a society that treated them as less than human, the family was where slaves grew and shared a culture of their own. Cultivating a marriage-based kinship under slavery was rebellion: a claim to humanity, an assertion of love.

It was also, in its bleak way, a privilege. Shirley A. Hill and other scholars have pointed out that the meticulous property records from large plantations might give a misleading idea of what constituted a 'normal' family life under slavery. Most slaves did not live on large plantations, and many did not live within close enough proximity to other slaveholding properties to form cross-plantation relationships. Because large plantations were a mark of wealth (hence, their rarity), slaves living on smaller plantations were likelier to be sold in moments of financial hardship, Hill writes. On small plantations, master-slave sexual relationships, early childbearing, and single-mother families were also far more common.

And while a prominent historical narrative emphasizes the efforts made by slave couples to reunite post-emancipation, Hill points out that the diversity of slave family experience, on account of economic difference, produced differing outcomes. Hill cites Lalita Tademy's *Cane River*, which uncovers that author's own family history, as evidence: 'Once slavery ended they scrambled to reunite their *families*, but not necessarily their *marriages*.' Nancy and Henry 'Box' Brown were damned; they were also, in the context of an institution that damned generations, perversely lucky to be able to choose, if fleetingly, each other.

In 1850, because life is nothing if not full of surprises, Irene Emerson – the widow of the Scotts' master – moved to Massachusetts and married known abolitionist and congressman Calvin C. Chaffee. As you might expect, the Supreme Court decision against Dred Scott wasn't exactly a boon to the Chaffee couple's reputation. The Chaffees transferred the Scott family to the son of Dred's former owner, who then filed manumission papers to free the Scott family on May 26, 1857. Dred Scott died a year and a half later, of tuberculosis. Harriet lived nearly two decades longer, and died in 1876. Some of their descendants are reported to live in St. Louis to this day.

'The "Flapper" Has Her Turn,' reads a *New York Times* headline from February 8, 1917, heralding a spring fashion breakthrough that would turn the city on its head. The announcement comes from the business section, a textile industry report nestled among others; in the same newspaper section, equal column inches are given, respectively, to a dispatch on inflated wool prices and another on the profit perils of poorly cast showroom models. But there's a knowing giddiness setting this trend-alert piece apart. Finally, the report goes, 'girls of the intermediate or "flapper" size' – grown women with skinny, boyish frames – would have 'every reason to congratulate themselves this season on the kind of things the local manufacturers are turning out for them to wear.' After years of neglect, a new cohort of stylish young women, of a certain age and build, would be able to purchase clothing made with their narrower figures in mind, straight from their favourite shops. Something else was happening, too: while the fabrics used for these women's new, ready-to-wear dresses would be 'practically a counterpart of the materials their older sisters are wearing,' they would be offered in 'the straight line silhouette' that was starting to grace the shops of Paris, courtesy of a young designer named Coco Chanel. The future had arrived in Manhattan's garment district, and the *New York Times* was on it.

There is a tendency to romanticize the 1920s as an age of sexual liberation that sprung fully formed, like Zeus, from the ashes of the Great War. The flapper – fortified by jazz, whisky pulled from garter flasks, economic prosperity, return other than, perhaps, the satisfaction of fulfilling what was expected of her. As her husband's yield increased, so did her workload. 'The average farmer's wife is one of the most patient and overworked women of the time,' marvelled an 1884 essay in the *American Farmer*. The same essay also noted that, of the 558 women admitted into the Connecticut Hospital for the Insane since its inception, 215 were housewives – 'and of course for the most part the wives of farmers.'

Lacking skills beyond the so-called household arts, the farmer's wife had limited economic recourse in the unfortunate event of death or abandonment; if her husband mistreated her or took to the bottle, as a good number unfortunately did, the best she might be able to hope for was succumbing to the tuberculosis or fatal childbirth that released so many other women of her day from their own, unending drudgery.

The rise of mass production, with the massive amount of minimally skilled labour it required, opened a door for women's entry to the world of waged work. By the late 1880s it was often cheaper and faster to buy bread than to bake it, and canned foods had become an affordable, time-saving staple of most households. Ready-made clothing was also becoming standard, and priced within reach of all but the lowest-positioned on the economic ladder. Commercial laundry facilities expanded in prevalence by 50 to 100 per cent with each decade between 1870 and 1910, and the number of women they employed increased accordingly. With so much time saved on domestic duties, and factories clamouring for female labour, unmarried daughters were all but redundant in their parental homes. As a result, many of them simply left.

Three-quarters of these wage-earning women were single, partly because single women had greater incentive to work, but also because of the expectation that a married woman shouldn't have to. The wide-eyed farm girl's journey from field to factory – and swift descent from innocence – was a fascination of yellow journalists and literary realists alike, immortalized by characters like the protagonist of Theodore Dreiser's 1900 novel *Sister Carrie*. Right from the book's opening page, Dreiser's omniscient (and very judgy) narrator reflects the era's hand-wringing paternalism over young working women. 'When a girl leaves her home at eighteen, she does one of two things,' he wrote. 'Either she falls into saving hands and becomes better, or she rapidly assumes the cosmopolitan standard of virtue and becomes worse.'

The novel goes on to follow eighteen-year-old Carrie's affairs with Chicago's moneyed older men, who gift her with fine meals, theatre tickets, and sophisticated wardrobes as she sheds the remaining traces of her hayseed past, compromising her morals in exchange for material goods and opportunities. She swaps the toil of the factory floor for the superficial glamours of a kept woman, picking up a bit theatre role through her lover's connections before making off with a different, married man. She eventually ends up a wildly successful stage actress in New York, earning $150 per week – over $4,000 in today's US dollars. Meanwhile her now-estranged husband (the formerly rich, formerly married-to-someone-else lover) fades in a flophouse. Carrie's a model of the American dream, and she's miserable.

In broad strokes, Dreiser's protagonist sent a cautionary message to a burgeoning middle class about the potential moral cost of ambition. But likely more immediately stirring, among contemporary readers, was Carrie's reflection of the widely held fear that single young women entering the city on their own would find themselves overwhelmed by the oh-so-alluring frivolities of urban life, and relinquish their integrity to obtain them.

But fear of change doesn't do much to curb it. As country folk continued to flock to cities, European immigrants arrived in droves. From 1880 to 1920, the number of foreign-born Americans doubled from nearly 7 million to just under 14 million. The bulk of these newcomers settled into the same Northeastern and Midwestern cities that were developing into hubs of manufacturing. By 1900, an estimated three-quarters of the populations of many large industrial cities – including New York, Chicago, San Francisco, Milwaukee, and Detroit – belonged to the immigrant community of either first- or second-generation Americans. A 1920 Census Bureau report confirmed that the US was no longer a nation of small farms: 51 per cent of Americans were now dwelling in cities, eking out an urban majority for the first time in American history.

The growing class of working women were employed by factories and offices, the department stores that clothed businessmen and the restaurants that fed them. Some toiled in laundries, others in wealthy families' homes as nannies or maids. Some were sex workers, some cabaret performers. Following the turn of the twentieth century, the expanded clerical sector employed more than one in three new female workers between 1900 and 1915, and raised the average working woman's full-time salary to just over half that of the average man. And whatever the job, single women made their own money and, in cities across the US, boarding houses multiplied to accommodate them affordably –

and to offer previously unimaginable levels of privacy convenient for conducting intimate affairs.

The grim reality of the market economy was that the road to relative freedom for some women was paved with the exploitation of other women's labour. Female wage earners could expect to be paid half as much as their male counterparts if they were lucky enough to have clerical work, and far less if employed on factory floors. The garment industry in particular was notorious for its meagrely paid female workforce – of which the majority were immigrant women – whose scanty salaries accompanied gruelling hours and taskmaster bosses.

The calamitous Triangle Shirtwaist Factory fire, which killed 146 New York City garment workers in 1911 and remains one of the deadliest industrial disasters in US history, drew into sharp relief the steep human cost of cheap consumer goods. Its workers, mostly Italian and Jewish immigrant women, could expect to earn between $7 and $12 for a fifty-two-hour workweek, less than $300 in today's currency. Many perished from smoke inhalation or, horribly, by flinging themselves out the burning factory's windows and onto the Greenwich Village street below, the workroom doors having been illegally locked shut by the factory proprietors to prevent the women from taking breaks. The disaster galvanized women's unionization movements and a sharp re-evaluation of workers' safety regulations. The woman's workday shortened from the ten to seventeen hours typical in 1885 to under ten by 1914, opening a space in young women's lives for the pursuit of leisure.

In tandem with a growing movement for worker rights, Congress authorized a 1911 report of the female labour force after three years of data collection. Helen L. Sumner, an economist who studied women's suffrage and labour, authored the ninth volume of the Senate report *History of Women in Industry in the United States*, which shed necessary light on the wage inequality and long hours working women were forced to endure. Sumner also made some basic observations about the social implications of women at work that drew an explicit connection between women's economic participation and the gendered changes in social convention that were raising the ire of conservative moralists:

> It is evident that on the whole there has been a certain expansion of woman's sphere – a decrease in the proportion employed in certain traditional occupations, such as 'servants and waitresses,' 'seamstresses,' and 'textile workers,' but an increase in the proportion employed in most other industries, many of them not originally considered as within woman's domain … [T]his movement has affected, roughly speaking, all elements, according to nativity or conjugal education, of the population of working women.

Sumner alluded to the increasingly porous boundary between men's and women's work as one cause for what pearl-clutchers might describe as the working woman's loss of innocence. At the very least, the woman's domain was changing in ways beyond even what could be plainly observed walking through city streets. But, of course, in practice, working women's adoption of new social mores was hardly so straightforward.

By and large, women of the labouring classes yearned to be seen – in spite of their possibly solitary dwellings and, perhaps, contact with single men – as decorous members of society, and certainly not as troublemakers.

Beginning in the 1890s, thousands of women joined clubs in cities throughout the US that served as hubs of like-minded community, civic participation, and personal enrichment. Some were aimed at well-to-do women for the purpose of coordinating well-meaning, if often patronizing, social volunteer efforts among the mostly immigrant ranks of the urban poor. African American women established their own organizations, such as the National Association of Colored Women's Clubs in 1896, whose motto 'Lifting as We Climb' sought to teach 'an ignorant and suspicious world that our aims and interests are identical with those of all good aspiring women.' Many other clubs were dedicated spaces for (white) 'working girls' to make friends, take on civic enrichment projects, and carve out a place for themselves in a rapidly changing society.

An 1890 issue of *Harper's Bazaar* reports that at a meeting of one such club, members discussed ways in which to improve their image. Solutions bandied about included gaining the respect of their employers by doing quality work ('if the average quality of work goes up, public opinion in regard to it will rise in proportion'); working to 'improve and cultivate our minds'; and careful conduct with the opposite sex ('A girl or woman who permits familiarity from boys or men may cause much annoyance to other girls for each is responsible, not only for herself, but for others'). While so much about the working woman's existence seemed to flout traditional conventions of femininity, it's likely that the average low-wage factory worker would have preferred not to be held as a model for the feminist vanguard. She wanted what, ultimately, most women did: to marry, raise a family, and leave the wage-labour force behind without a backward glance.

At the same time, a new kind of self-assured and independent woman had begun to make her mark among the upper classes of urbanized European and American society. Unlike her working-class sisters, this privileged woman's liberated existence wasn't a by-product of new-found self-sufficiency from (relatively) low-wage labour but, rather, a rebellion against the social mores that had previously dictated upper-class women's behaviour. The timing, however, was far from coincidental.

For generations, wealthy married women had been expected to do little other than raise children and maintain their households – or, more precisely, to manage the domestic staff that did the bulk of both. But by the late 1800s, most upper-class homes had a gas line to power light and heat, which meant no more hauling of wood and coal, and no more scrubbing of their sooty residues. Some homes even had their own water, washing away the cumulative hours spent visiting local pumps and hauling water back to the household, bucket by individual bucket. Laundry facilities eliminated the burden of daily wash, a physically gruelling and time-intensive activity. In turn, wealthy households didn't need as many staff to keep their estates running smoothly. With little else to do, the matrons of these homes became painfully bored, even manifesting the symptoms we would now associate with depression.

The New Woman, as christened by the Irish feminist author Sarah Grand, emerged as a Gilded Age response to the misery produced by a culture that demanded polite uselessness of its well-to-do women. The New Woman, Grand proposed, embodied part of an awakening from her sex's docile complicity in her own subjugation. She was boldly demanding better from men, but also more for herself.

The New Woman was, if not directly involved in the burgeoning suffrage movement, tacitly influenced by its momentum. She may have had a university education, in spite of the social consequences; in the 1870s and 1880s, the number of coeducational and women's-only universities in the US swelled, though 75 per cent of those who graduated before 1900 would never marry. Or maybe she'd already been married and was now living on her own; thanks to the recent developments in matrimonial legislation that would allow her to retain her assets in the event of a divorce, a potential ex-husband wasn't out of the question.

The outspoken, educated feminists of the upper class were an object of fascination in fin de siècle literature and, equally, fodder for public outcry. Men and women had previously occupied clearly delineated spheres: men in public, women in the home, with little cross-gender interaction outside of the family. As women rejected their designated domestic stations, they threatened what was, for many, a foundation of social order.

Though the 'Woman Question' jostled the collective consciousness, the intense aversion to women's pursuit of public personhood hardly made a case for maintaining the status quo. The so-called 'Bawling Brotherhood' protested against the social infiltration of women, reflected in Basil Ransom's protestations that '[t]he whole generation is womanized' and 'if we don't look out, will usher in the reign of mediocrity,' in Henry James's 1886 novel *The Bostonians*. No matter: women were tired of being held back, understimulated, and miserable. If men were unwilling to recognize women's autonomy, that was on them.

The New Women of the Gilded Age, by and large, comprised a group of women whose class status afforded them both the opportunity and the entitlement to ruffle feathers. This feminist movement included few working-class women – not because poor women didn't desire fair treatment, but rather the circumstances of urban poverty and gruesome working conditions posed more immediate concerns than the finer points of the Woman Question. Put another way, the New Woman could literally afford to run her mouth, trusting that there would still be food for her to put in it.

Still, despite the limitations in her perspective, the Gilded Age feminist's position of socio-economic advantage would prove useful in setting a framework for what women might deign to strive for. The New Women were, after all, sufficiently distant from the basic quandaries of daily economic survival to allow for analysis – their own and everyone else's – of what women's changing roles might mean. They were uniquely positioned to even *endeavour to suggest* that male and female detractors of the women's movement were, respectively, babies and cowards. The New Woman had the socio-political influence to address the socio-political implications of the collapse into one another of men's and women's spheres, and to suggest that society's fixed notions of men, women, and the family could become unfixed. It was the New Woman who could confront the Woman Question: what was a woman, if not defined in relation to a man?

Moralists argued that it was for women's own good to force their exclusion from public, enfranchised, wage-earning society. But as the free market proliferated, feminist writers like Charlotte Perkins Gilman flipped the script on moralistic hand-wringing in favour of the New Woman's cause. Gilman argued in her 1898 treatise *Women and*

Economics that, by positioning marriage and motherhood as the only acceptable occupations for women, a society that so scorned the 'vice' of prostitution was hypocritically selling marriage as a version of the same: 'We are the only animal species in which the female depends on the male for food, the only animal species in which the sex-relation is also an economic relation.'

Just over a decade later, the anarchist Emma Goldman would pose a similar argument in her seminal 1910 essay, 'The Traffic in Women.' Here she is quoting the influential nineteenth-century British sexologist Havelock Ellis:

> The wife who married for money, compared with the prostitute, is the true scab. She is paid less, gives much more in return in labor and care, and is absolutely bound to her master. The prostitute never signs away the right over her own person, she retains her freedom and personal rights, nor is she always compelled to submit to a man's embrace.

As scholars of vice in the US have pointed out, the female sex workers who were the contemporaries of Gilman and Goldman had more money and personal freedom than any other women in America. 'In fact,' writes author Thaddeus Russell in his 2010 *A Renegade History of the United States*, 'prostitutes won virtually all the freedoms that were denied to women but are now taken for granted … Prostitutes made, by far, the highest wages of all American women.' Wax your moustaches on that, Progressive Era assholes.

The threat of sexual misconduct weighed heavily on the minds of polite society and civic leaders alike, and it nagged over a span of decades. Ambient unease over women's sexual corruption pervaded the middle and upper classes in cities from London to New York. On both sides

the writer Mary Augusta Laselle eyed such superficial airs with great suspicion. 'The working girl's hat, shoes, dress, and general attire are in too many cases a fantastic imitation of the costly costumes of women of large incomes,' Laselle wrote in 1914, a condescension in line with the commonly held belief that working-class women were hoping to rise in social ranks by luring wealthier husbands. Whether or not that particular motivation for 'putting on style' was exactly fair or accurate, there were certainly dating-market advantages to keeping up appearances.

Dating also offered both men and women a new-found freedom to try out the affections of a partner – or several – without necessarily heading straight for the aisle. Facilitated by the free market, the advent of dating threw a new layer of capitalist competition into the quest for companionship. Women donned ready-to-wear fashions and powdered their noses with cosmetics they paid for, with money all their own, in service of standing out in the crowd of competing single dames. Inadvertently, they primed the culture for a character that would embody the reckless exuberance of new romance.

By the 1920s, the public's perception of the type of young woman who went on 'dates' was nearly synonymous with the caricature of the flapper: a short-skirted libertine who flouted the conventions of all the women who'd come before her. This woman was an object of fixation and ridicule; she racked up boyfriends in her off-the-rack sheath dresses and lacquered hairdos, doing who knows what with them behind closed doors. But, not unlike the scaffolding she pieced together from department-store fashions, she was also largely a fictive ideal to be consumed.

Skidmore College professor emerita of English Linda Simon argues in *Lost Girls: The Invention of the Flapper* that the physical ideal of the flapper emerged in part from the massive popularity of Peter Pan, a boy permanently frozen in adolescence and always played onstage by a woman. Her short skirts and impossibly straight-lined sinews were etched into existence by the prolific illustrator John Held Jr.'s covers for the likes of *Vanity Fair* and *Life* magazines in the 1920s, and the dust jackets for F. Scott Fitzgerald's *Tales of the Jazz Age* (1922) and *The Vegetable* (1923). Cosmetic manufacturers leapt at the fetishization of youth and slenderness that the flapper so embodied – dieting came into fashion, and business boomed for girdle makers and cosmetic surgeons. The flapper, in other words, was a commodity: an idea to be bought and sold.

Many young women ascribed to this ideal. Despite early excitement in its business pages, the *New York Times* was slow to laud the modern woman of the 1920s – or, at least, knew to milk a good controversy when it saw one. In a 1921 letter to the editor that praised one of the paper's recent stories, a young Edith M. Mendel (who would later become a pioneering advocate for mental health and disability rights under her married name, Edith M. Stern) countered her positive feedback with the assertion that 'as a college senior, a flapper and a feminist, naturally I do not usually subscribe to your Victorian attitude toward women.'

A 1922 *New York Times* article, 'More Ado about the Flapper,' defined the newly liberated young woman largely in relation to her dating habits. This was a woman who led a mysterious double life, who would be 'engaged more or less seriously upon other concerns' during the day before flitting into the night with a revolving legion of dancing partners. The *Times*'s rhetoric in this piece also not-so-subtly aligns the practice of dating with the sale of sex: 'The purpose of their flapping is collecting – collecting and still collecting – a male clientele – in short, beaux.'

One of the article's subjects is the acclaimed stage and screen actress Laurette Taylor. Taylor, who by 1922 was approaching forty, dismissed the flapper as a 'little rich girl.' When countered with the suggestion that maybe single women on the dating market included independent gals with ordinary jobs, Taylor scoffed: 'I don't call those flappers. They are fast young persons. A good girl would be content with one man. She would collect him and begin her real job. Your flapper – if you can call her that – can't work or study all day and dance all night and make good at what she works at.'

As is still true today, young women were the dispro-portionate targets of public scorn over a cultural shift that also, equally, pertained to men. The flapper wasn't exactly out there dancing by herself. Further, there was no panic over the figure of the kind of man who went on 'dates'; no one saw him as somehow an amoral aberration rather than an individual simply playing his part in a change in the tides. And despite the dismissive sneers of so many Laurette Taylors, the tides were definitely changing … with sexy results.

In his 1928 survey of one hundred married men and one hundred married women born before 1900, psychiatrist G. V. Hamilton found that 67 per cent of women born from 1886 to 1890 were virgins at marriage, as opposed to only 30 per cent of the same number of women born from 1891 to 1900. One hundred respondents may not constitute a scientific sample size, but it does hint at a trend with some momentum. Other studies supported the phenomenon, estimating that half of all college-educated women had engaged in premarital sex – and 21 per cent of women, regardless of education, by age twenty – by the 1920s.

Premarital sex also carried an economic connotation. Among working-class women whose wages were barely enough to survive on, sex offered a bartering tool to exchange for middle-class 'treats,' like movies and dinners, that their better-compensated male dates would be able to provide. At the Bureau of Social Hygiene's 'laboratory' at the Bedford reformatory, many of the women inmates interviewed insisted they had been wrongfully accused of prostitution – they had never sold sex for money. Rather, as one woman reported, they went on dates with male friends who might offer trips 'to Coney Island to dances and Picture Shows.'

In addition to the odd evening out, young women were also beginning to discover that sex was something they *liked*. '[S]moking, dancing like Voodoo devotees, dressing décolleté, "petting" and drinking, we do these things because we honestly enjoy the attendant physical sensations,' explained a 1922 co-ed in the Ohio State University *Lantern*. 'We are "playing the game."' The more things change, the more they stay the same.

At the time, acknowledging that sex was something women could actively desire, rather than enter into out of a grudging Victorian sense of marital obligation, was considered … impolite. But attitudes were changing. Influential writings by Sigmund Freud and Havelock Ellis (who, in addition to providing Emma Goldman with an endlessly quotable quip likening marriage to the sale of sex, was years ahead of his time in proposing that both homosexuality and women's sexual desire were far from aberrations) were beginning to popularize the idea that sexual desire was an essential component of the human psyche (which was itself subject to a growing amount of interest), and popular culture backed it up.

For example, consider Eleanor Savage. The suggestively named flapper debutante of F. Scott Fitzgerald's *This Side of Paradise* initially bonds with Fitzgerald's male protagonist/personal stand-in over their shared love of literary dissection. But as she emerges as a potential love interest, she reveals a seen-it-all flavour of romantic jadedness that speaks for the modern woman of the day – or at least, à la Fitzgerald, her rough approximation:

> I like clever men and good-looking men, and, of course, no one cares more for personality than I do. Oh, just one person in fifty has any glimmer of what sex is. I'm hipped on Freud and all that, but it's rotten that every bit of *real* love in the world is ninety-nine per cent passion and one little soupçon of jealousy.

Eleanor Savage may not have been real, but she was onto something. Until this point in Anglo memory, there hadn't been a whole lot of attention given to the importance of women's sexual pleasure.

Married Love, a 1918 treatise by the British scientist Marie Stopes, changed that. Stopes's book was one of the first popular texts to propose that women's sexual desire was not only natural and universal, but an attribute that husbands would do well to attend to. Stopes didn't mince words; most men entered into marriage not knowing how to sexually satisfy a woman, while most women didn't grasp what the sexual encounter should entail. Stopes describes how sex should involve a real pleasure 'which should sweep over every wife each time she and her husband unite. The key which unlocks this electric force in his wife must reverently be sought by every husband.' In the same breath, Stopes made the bold hypothesis that men who had lost their virginity to prostitutes prior to getting married were inclined to mistake their paid sex partner's yawps and quivers for a testament to their own sexual prowess; these same men were also likely, in turn, to blame their future wives' lack of sexual arousal on what they perceived was her frigidity instead of their own shortcomings in the sack. (A hubristic misconception that many straight women would surely affirm has stood the test of time.)

Married Love sold out so swiftly that it would be reprinted five times within two weeks of its release. Its content was considered so threatening that the US Customs Service banned its American circulation for thirteen years, and not just because people were terrified to consider the meaning of sex. Women's sexual agency was a disconcerting prospect, particularly when coupled with her burgeoning economic agency. When not under tight social control, what was to become of the family unit upon which a capitalist economy and Judeo-Christian moral order were both, simultaneously, contingent and upheld?

One answer was a new relationship model that demanded an implicit rejection of the values that had governed Western society for millennia: that is, the idea that marriage could be designed to fulfill the companionate and sexual needs of men and women first and foremost. Sexuality, within the regulatory confines of a state-sanctified marriage, would be embraced and even celebrated. Most people found the prospect utterly terrifying.

Life's Short. Get a Divorce.

The twenties roared, until they didn't. The stock market crash of 1929 put an end to Jazz Age frivolity and, for a time, kept people from severing their relationships and the security those relationships provided. Pragmatism had always lurked in the wings, but the desperation of the Depression thrust it to centre stage.

The century leading up to the crash was one of pure momentum. Technology advanced and cities grew; slavery ended and women across racial lines became legally recognized as individuals. Circumstances were far from perfect – far, for many, from satisfactory (it's worth noting, for one, that Black women were blocked from voting in some southern states through the 1960s). But, by and large, women gained rights that cleared a culturally unprecedented plane of legal and logistical autonomy. The redistribution of capital across gender lines was its primary driver. With the scarcity of Depression came precaution. The divorce rate, which had risen steadily for the last half-century and spiked over the 1920s, dropped by 25 per cent in the US between 1929 and 1933. The rate of marriage correspondingly plummeted by 22 per cent, as a lack of employment disincentivized the creation of new families. And then the Great Depression was followed immediately by war. Women again surged into the workforce, some by supplanting newly appointed servicemen in traditionally male industries like aviation and munitions. An estimated 40 per cent of American women went to work. Women who had never before imagined themselves in the position of supporting their families remained rare. The car-dependent design of new community developments, which aimed in large part to keep out racialized city dwellers who relied on public transit, also kept the women living inside from leaving.

Suburban motherhood was a trip. And yet, women's memory of what once had been wasn't lost. The wives and mothers of the mid-twentieth century were the daughters of women who had fought for the right to vote, had themselves taken men's jobs during the war and gotten university degrees. Amid the baby boom and suburbanization of the family, married women began to re-enter the workforce almost immediately – a reality that's sometimes lost behind the dominant residual memory of the 1950s housewife.

Of course, whether conflicted or content, the housewife did occupy an outsize role in the culture of the time. As the age of postwar domesticity developed, a long-held feminist mistrust of marital convention was thrust back into the fore of a reawakened women's movement that would expand the discussion of women's equality into the workplace and home. In *The Second Sex*, first published in 1949 and widely considered to have laid the foundation for feminism's second wave, Simone de Beauvoir positions the contemporary marriage as a near-inevitable force for women's spiritual annihilation. A housewife's contribution to the household served not to instill her with the fortitude of duty or satisfaction over useful contribution, but to highlight the degree to which she was dependent on others for validation.

'[A housewife's work] becomes meaningful and dignified only if it is integrated into existences that go beyond themselves, toward the society in production or action,' de Beauvoir wrote. 'Far from enfranchising the matron, it makes her dependent on her husband and children; she justifies her existence through them: she is no more than an inessential meditation in their lives.'

In some ways, de Beauvoir's trapped housewife presented a new iteration of a classic trope of bourgeois preoccupation. The cloistered madwoman, made desperate by the constraints of domesticity, had ached her way through gothic literary narratives from Brontë to Gilman nearly a century prior. The difference, perhaps, was that the domestic malaise of the mid-twentieth-century middle class became enshrouded in the kinds of material comforts that can make existential strife more complicated to pin down. Life, on the whole, wasn't necessarily all that bad for the dependent housewife. She was provided for; the chores she attended to were made breezy by an assortment of new housekeeping technologies, like the washing machine and the vacuum cleaner. Practically speaking, the desperate housewife's mother had likely had it much worse.

Then again, ennui thrives in stillness. The very appliances that had come to rescue the 1950s wife and mother facilitated moments of dangerous quiet. In lieu of back-breaking labour, she could be introspective. Women instinctively knew this; so, too, did the companies that profited from them. 'The hidden attitude of women toward labor-saving devices is decidedly surprising,' writes journalist Vance Packard in 'The Ad and the Id,' a feature in a 1957 *Harper's Bazaar*.

> Working wives can accept them, but the full-time housewife is liable to feel that they threaten her importance and creativity. The research director of an ad agency sadly explained the situation as follows: 'If you tell the housewife that by using your washing machine, drier or dishwasher she can

be free to play bridge, you're dead! – the housewife today
already feels guilty about the fact that she is not working as
hard as her mother.'

Despite being tasked with the unpaid labour that kept the household running, the housewife did not want to diminish her own sense of usefulness. She wanted to matter.

The restless unease of many middle-class housewives was crystalized in Betty Friedan's *The Feminine Mystique* (1963); reading Friedan marked, for these housewives, the first glimmer of recognition that they were not uniquely broken. According to Friedan, the housewife's quiet turmoil was felt equally among women whose husbands were struggling at low-paying jobs and those who brought home hefty salaries. '[T]he problem that has no name,' Friedan wrote,

stirring in the minds of so many American women today is not a matter of loss of femininity or too much education, or the demands of domesticity … We can no longer ignore that voice within women that says: 'I want something more than my husband and my children and my home.'

Friedan's feminist hand grenade had developed from a years-long journalistic investigation, but the frustrations that her case studies vocalized hit close to home. Friedan herself had turned down a graduate fellowship in the mid-1940s to preserve a relationship with a boyfriend who'd felt threatened by her academic success. She would later explain that she'd chosen as she had to avoid 'becoming an old maid college teacher.' The boyfriend became her husband and, by the end of the 1960s, her ex-husband.

Many of Friedan's early critics, both male and female, derided the author's implication that being a housewife was a somehow inadequate occupation of a woman's time. In *A Strange Stirring: 'The Feminine Mystique' and American Women at the Dawn of the 1960s*, Stephanie Coontz reports that the magazine *Ladies' Home Journal* received hundreds of letters from readers after publishing an excerpt from *The Feminine Mystique* in advance of its publication, 80 per cent of them angry. In the decades since, Friedan's elitism – evidenced through her specific prescription of creative, intellectually stimulating work – and homophobia have garnered detractors of their own.

Nevertheless, some readers of the era would argue that *The Feminine Mystique* had infused in them the fortitude to leave marriages already in distress. Coontz reports how eye-opening Friedan's argument had been for many of its middle-class, white women readers. One married mother of two who, in 1963 and 1964, read the book 'in pieces and parts when time permitted,' credits Friedan for allowing her to envision a life beyond her cramped domestic bubble. By arguing that women could claim an identity beyond their miserable marriages, the reader credits Friedan for giving her 'the right to divorce.' She later remarried a long-time friend whom she'd known since high school, 'who is and was the love of my life.' The blissful remarriage, Coontz writes, is a common narrative thread among the post-*Mystique* divorcees she's surveyed. Once granted the informal permission to become active participants in their own relationships – and, by extension, the daily structure of their own lives – many women found themselves in relationships that fulfilled them.

The Feminine Mystique never makes an argument against marriage, per se. Unlike *The Second Sex* – in almost every respect the more anti-establishment work and almost certainly intended for an audience of like-minded intellectuals – *The Feminine Mystique* was as much self-help manual as manifesto. Friedan's book remains the touchstone of the era precisely because its readers were *not* activists or academics. They were, instead, the middle-class women who gathered housekeeping advice from women's magazines and swore by the guidelines of paperback parenting guru Dr. Spock.

The book gives voice to a specific feeling, and supplies evidence that the feeling is widely shared. Before Friedan, nobody had quite articulated the precariousness of crafting an entire adult identity on the bases of marriage and motherhood, nor offered a potential curative (in this case, personal goals and a path to pursuing them). Its first printing alone sold 1.4 million copies.

The alternative to what Friedan had identified as 'the problem with no name' was women's participation in traditionally male spheres – more precisely, secured status as equal actors in the workforce and marketplace. It's easy to see why Friedan's abridged prognosis took hold among Anglo middle- and upper-class readers – her solution doesn't destabilize the capitalist mechanics of class and wealth; it just provides a certain cohort of women with the right to desire to participate as fully as the men they'd known their entire lives. As many have pointed out in the decades that followed *The Feminine Mystique*, Friedan's tome erased not only the economic and structural forces that guaranteed women's ongoing oppression, but the author's own history as a labour organizer and radical leftist journalist.

Friedan had spent the decade from 1942 to 1952 working for union publications, first as a reporter for the labour-news syndicator Federated Press, and then for seven years as a staff writer with the magazine of the United Electrical, Radio, and Machine Workers of America. Decades later, the historian Daniel Horowitz would lament *The Feminine Mystique*'s omission of both Friedan's past and the movement she'd spent ten years covering: '[I]t was a loss to American history that a remarkable journalist and feminist leader failed to bring forward the seminal contributions that labor ideals and struggles had made to feminism in the twentieth century.'

Loss or no, the individual rather than collectivist focus of *The Feminine Mystique* was likely by design. It may have been for the benefit of her intended audience that Friedan centred her critique on the pursuit of individual happiness, as opposed to the economic freedom required to buttress such a lofty objective. The blame for mid-century familial discord was often placed squarely on wives – a consequence, Friedan argued, of the so-called feminine mystique. The wife of an unhappy husband needed only to will his happiness into being, and it would be so; the husband whose sexual appetites had wandered outside of his marriage could refocus his interests on marital satisfaction, and in turn he'd be cured of temptation. As Cherlin's study points out, however, the mounting pressure to be happy in marriage would come to outweigh the potential costs of leaving behind a relationship that wasn't.

On New Year's Day of 1971, a new law went into effect that would completely change the nature of divorce in the state of California. Signed by then-governor Ronald Reagan, the legislation narrowed the litany of potential grounds for marital dissolution to just two: 'incurable insanity' and something called 'irreconcilable differences.' The latter divorced, as opposed to roughly half of American kids born two decades later.

And as the rate of divorce surged, so shifted the cultural perception of how children fit into the equation. Throughout the 1950s and into the early years of the following decade, bad marriages were likely to be met with an ethos of 'stay-together-for-the-kids.' William Strauss and Neil Howe's 1991 demographic compendium, *Generations*, reports that in 1962, half of adult women held the stoic belief that unhappy marriages ought to be toughed out until the children had flown the nest.

But the rising belief that success and happiness were self-driven outcomes, which so shaped family life of the 1950s, also fostered a cultural climate that would make the divorce revolution possible. The social-hygiene preoccupations that had dogged the well-to-do at the turn of the century had been replaced, post–World War II, by a self-improvement bent that primed the public for a deluge of psychobabble. Self-help books sold by the millions and helped to support the belief that nothing couldn't be solved with the application of a little elbow grease and a good Protestant work ethic.

The Power of Positive Thinking, a 1952 pop-psychology bestseller written by Norman Vincent Peale (a Methodist-ordained minister who had no formal background in psychology and would later go on to spiritually advise the Trump family), argued that couples who were tempted to part ways needed only to approach their relationship with new resolve. If they obsessively meditated on a concrete image of shared happiness, eventually that vision would materialize as though their collective denial had been cosmically repurposed as an incantation.

Peale gave the example of a woman whose husband wanted a divorce. After setting aside her private inner 'hysteria' at the thought, she asked that her dissatisfied husband allow for a ninety-day grace period in which to reconsider. During that time, she worked diligently to conjure images of their happy golf outings together, to imagine him sitting in a favourite chair that seemed to be a stand-in for their marriage itself. It worked! After ninety days, he forgot he'd wanted a divorce at all – an outcome Peale assured readers he had seen many times in his role as a spiritual advisor. It was a compelling message for mid-century Americans, who were swallowing en masse the postwar illusion that their material successes were the product of individual labours – of opportunity and hard work – rather than a confluence of economic forces that had momentarily parted the curtains onto a window of growth that, by the early 1970s, would be shut forever.

Friedan's emphasis on labour as a means toward self-actualization ironically set up *The Feminine Mystique* as the housewife's answer to Peale's happiness how-to. In so doing, the book alienated many working-class and non-white women who had never been allotted the luxury of housewifehood to begin with. Non-white feminists have incidentally spent the past half-century pointing out the ways in which their ongoing economic participation has fallen short of white feminists' emancipatory promise. As the ground-breaking Black feminist theorist bell hooks points out in her 1984 book *Feminist Theory: From Margin to Center*, Friedan had effectively universalized the experience of 'a select group of college-educated, middle- and upper-class, married white women – housewives bored

Kids of the 1970s were being raised to believe that marriage was a worthwhile pursuit for love and partnership and not just a duty of life 'because it's what people do'; as such, journalists and experts helped circulate the idea that divorce could actually be *good* for them, insofar as they strengthened a mother's independence. A 1979 article in the *Marriage & Family Review* argued that divorce and subsequent remarriage might even hold 'capacities for growth and development' for mothers and create 'a larger network of effective kin ties' that would distribute the burden of emotional and economic caregiving.

During my research for this book, I'd punch 'divorce' into digital periodical databases and note what turned up – or, specifically, how it was different from what had turned up before, when my results had been confined within a different chronological window. It wasn't until the 1970s that the search yielded consistent hits beyond the occasional alarmist short story. I pulled up an excerpt from a children's non-fiction book about divorce reprinted in a 1971 issue of *Harper's Bazaar*, wherein a Dr. Richard Gardner introduces himself to young readers as a 'special kind of doctor who tries to help children who have trouble and worries.' The book is clearly meant to help children address their feelings about parental divorce head-on, rather than pretend nothing's the matter. 'If you've been doing this,' Gardner cautions underaged would-be stoics, 'now's the time to stop!' (Gardner later became obsessed with the idea that false accusations of child sexual abuse were a new social hysteria akin to the Puritan witch trials; his 2003 *New York Times* obituary would be notable in its verbatim reprint of a pro–Woody Allen screed against Mia Farrow during the couple's high-profile 1992 custody dispute, which hinged on Allen's alleged abuse of the pair's daughter Dylan. But that's a whole other story.)

Then and still today, women were, on the whole, much likelier than men to instigate divorce proceedings, which contemporary sociologists attribute to asymmetrical rates of marital dissatisfaction. Women are typically still disproportionately expected to carry the brunt of uncompensated – that is, mental, emotional, and domestic – labour, and it turns out that that's exhausting. (That a scant 20 per cent of married women keep their own surnames, as of a 2015 study commissioned by Google and the *New York Times*, might be cited as evidence of said exhaustion – not because women shouldn't be allowed to call themselves whatever they like, but because, according to Stanford sociology professor Michael Rosenfeld, it's apparently not uncommon for men to pressure their fiancées into making the switch.)

But while the women's liberation movement was gaining momentum alongside these legislative changes, women's increased social and economic autonomy were not likely its primary drivers. The fact was, as the nature of marriage itself continued its evolution from a religiously binding property agreement to comprising one of a few more facets of self-actualization, there was less incentive to stay in one that was unhappy. And, if there were children involved, the no-fault divorce placed less onus on the male partner to fork over the bulk of his assets to care for his estranged family. It was mutually beneficial for both partners involved; wives no longer had to deliver a judicial play-by-play of their suffering, and husbands were relieved of the financial burden the former system would have placed.

Though the family unit isn't at risk of becoming obsolete, it's certainly undergoing a period of transition. Premarital cohabitation has risen steadily since the 1970s; more than 65 per cent of young adult couples in the US will live together before the exchange of 'I do,' and nearly four out of ten will never get to the proverbial altar at all. Statistics Canada opted in 2011 to stop collecting data on marriage and divorce rates altogether, citing the changing nature of relationship definitions as motivation for the cost-saving move.

In a single generation, partnership configurations that were considered transgressive not that long ago have become dully commonplace. I feel like a relic when recounting the acronym POSSLQ, for 'person of opposite sex sharing living quarters,' which was coined by the US Census Bureau at the end of the 1970s and used with regularity through my 1990s childhood. Within my own lifetime, introducing one's POSSLQ at a party signified a kind of vanguard status, a self-conscious deviation from the prescribed path. It was even a little pretentious, as exemplified by the character of Frasier Crane on the early-nineties sitcom *Cheers*, who used the term to describe his relationship to future wife Lilith. Now the word is all but forgotten.

No longer a census subcategory, cohabitating couples are merely – boringly – becoming a new norm. The number of unmarried couples living together has increased by a staggering 900 per cent in the last fifty years. Some 8 million American couples are living together unmarried, well over double the figure from twenty years ago. About half of those cohabiting adults are under thirty-five. 'Nowadays, want to, the biggest and most expensive party many of us will ever have. In 2016, wedding-related services amassed an estimated $72 billion in revenue in the US alone.

Ever since the ceremony between Diana Spencer and Charles, Prince of Wales, was broadcast to an international audience nearly four decades ago, getting married has become an opportunity to indulge in a massive amount of lifestyle spectacle. The TV show *Say Yes to the Dress* is premised entirely on future brides' selection of a bridal gown priced in the five figures; one of the most successful, long-running reality franchises on network TV ends with the 'winner' getting handpicked for marriage by an eligible bachelor or bachelorette.

Where a few centuries ago, our ancestors were warning against the perils of love within marriage, it's now the biggest reason people cite for getting hitched. A recent survey showed that love and 'making a lifelong commitment' outweighed having children and even religious recognition of a relationship as motives for marrying – a radical departure in priority from as recently as our grandparents' generation. And even lower on the list of marriage priorities, according to the survey, was money: only 28 per cent of respondents cited financial stability as a very important reason to get married, as opposed to the 88 per cent who said the same of love.

Still, marriage remains a major long-term determinant of financial security. It is also a reflection *of* economic security. In the US, middle- and lower-income men – that is, the demographic hit hardest by the decline in domestic manufacturing – have experienced the steepest decline in marriage rates since 1970, a slope that neatly parallels that group's drop in earning power.

At the same time, women on the lower- and middle-earning rungs of the economic ladder have fared much better over the past four decades than their male counterparts. Dual-income households are financially better off regardless of the gender configuration or who earns what.

As our domestic lives become – practically speaking – less dictated by old mores about men's and women's spheres and the contracts that bind them, our material circumstances leave women better equipped than ever to bounce back from a rupture in the nuclear family unit. But, despite ostensibly ample licence to leave a relationship when it no longer feels like the right place to be, we are maybe more predisposed than ever to make clumsy sense of our own romantic ambivalence.

Pummelled by a lifetime of social conditioning, we absorb messages that remain at odds with the practical realities of our humdrum day-to-days. We weigh a set of contradictory stakes when considering our love lives. This measuring of considerations and needs – physical, emotional, intellectual, psychological, financial, reproductive – can be crazy-making. The dissolution of a romantic relationship can become like a riddle with no clear solution.

In her 1995 novel *The End of the Story*, author Lydia Davis narrows in on the mythologizing tendency of recent romantic hindsight. Beginning the book with 'the end' of the affair, Davis's narrator endeavours on the project of retracing her broken relationship's steps to find the answer to the riddle, in reverse.

'How strange it is to realize now that although I was frightened of the emptiness between us, that emptiness was not his fault but mine: I was waiting to see what he would give me, how he would entertain me,' the female and mass proliferation of contraceptives further distanced sex from reproductive duty, simultaneously opening the door for queer relationships in public life. Late capitalism has set the conditions for our relative autonomy, while also ensuring that we play by its rules. And therein lies the rub.

By now, most mainstream feminists will, at the very least, pay lip service to the idea that capitalism is a paradoxical boon to our liberty and a pain in the ass – at once a potential tool for personal autonomy and the chain around our necks that systemically reinforces our reliance on the brokers of power. (Spoiler: white men!) 'Pink think' isn't the problem, though it might be dressing the window.

Yet, there's not total agreement on exactly *how* patriarchy and the market economy feed into one another. The prevailing thesis is, more or less, that capitalism relies on patriarchy and, by extension, a nuclear family wherein (traditionally) female-performed domestic labour is both necessary and monetarily unvalued. Patriarchy doesn't need capitalism, the argument goes, but capitalism does need patriarchy.

Prominent 1970s feminists like Kate Millett and Shulamith Firestone positioned patriarchy as a catch-all for male dominance in society, and capitalism as its squirrelly bedfellow. 'To make both women and children totally independent would be to eliminate not just the patriarchal nuclear family, but the biological family itself,' wrote Firestone in her 1970 book *The Dialectic of Sex: The Case for Feminist Revolution*. Firestone would also echo Marx's theory that the nuclear family formed the basis for the broader 'antagonisms' established within the state.

Yet others, like British academic Michèle Barrett, have argued that the 'needs' of capitalism don't fully account for women's oppression in contemporary society, in part because women's experiences are so varied and, also, because simple correlates between the two can gloss over women's oppression in pre-capitalist history, in socialist societies, and within different classes today.

At any rate, there's a demonstrable relationship between patriarchy and the current distribution of world power, which is also aligned with access to wealth. Wealth and power: the ultimate bedfellows. That white men are disproportionately in possession of both is a statistic reflected in places like Western legislative bodies and corporate boardrooms and, as you may have observed, just about everywhere else.

It's safe to propose that patriarchy is at least propped up by the current distribution of wealth and power, if not necessarily a product of it. I tend to side with Barrett: patriarchy as an ideology doesn't necessarily rely on capitalism – they just happen to be very complementary means of consolidating resource control in the hands of a select few.

Resources can, as much as anything, discourage the dissolution of a domestic partnership, particularly for the party with the most to lose. In a majority of couples, that means women. Roughly three-quarters of American households report a male breadwinner. Women in the US earn an average of 20 per cent less than men for full-time work, and even in countries like Canada and the UK, where women fare slightly better, they still earn an average of 13 per cent and 9.4 per cent less, respectively, than their male counterparts. Because women in all three countries are likelier than men to work part-time or contract jobs, the composite wage gap between all men and women workers is even wider. With age and child-rearing, the gap tends to widen still further.

Narrowing the gender pay gap is broadly cited as a key priority by mainstream feminists, a stance echoed by left-of-centre politicians and reflected in policy measures to support equal pay for equal work. Social conservatives, on the other hand, are likelier to argue that the disparity is overstated and that, furthermore, women are simply more inclined to enter into lower-paying professions.

Whatever its root causes, the gender wage gap is almost certainly informed – and maintained – by social biases. Some women may prefer to steer clear of testosterone-driven occupations like trading for cultural reasons, just as some employers may, consciously or otherwise, decide that a new male hire is worth a higher starting salary than his equally qualified female counterpart. In any event, there remains a lingering belief that one of the most important roles a man can serve is as his family's provider. In the US, a 2013 report from the Pew Research Center found that while 41 per cent of respondents agreed that providing income for his children was one of a father's top responsibilities, only 25 per cent felt the same of mothers.

Queer women aren't exempt from the combined ambiguity of cultural expectation and economic reality, different though their specific challenges may be. Ruth Schwartz, relationship counsellor, co-founder of the dating site Conscious Girlfriend, and co-author of two books on lesbian relationships, told me, 'Biologically, our brains are crammed full of ideas about how to do partner selection that have to do with survival of the species and nothing to do with what most of us psychologically want and prefer and need at this point in our evolution as human beings, in this privileged culture.'

Schwartz and partner/co-author Michelle Murrain launched Conscious Girlfriend to help queer women identify the conflicting signals between biological impulses and emotional needs – something that straight-leaning women might have a leg up on, thanks to a lifetime of expecting to conflate the two. These are the mixed internal signals that lead queer women to enter into relationships with the wrong partners, or to find themselves poorly equipped to adjust to the demands of a relationship after the initial period of limerence – the borderline-psychotic period of biochemical fuckery commonly known as 'the honeymoon phase' – wears off.

I asked Schwartz whether some version of the 'rare good man' exists in queer communities, some self-sabotaging mythos that has just enough basis in reality to persist (and make life difficult). Is queer love the way to dodge the sticky effects of patriarchy in partnership? Does the trauma of being part of a marginalized community defined by the nature of your sexuality establish a different, yet comparably toxic, set of pitfalls?

She replied with a joke: 'What does a lesbian bring on the second date? A U-Haul!' I'd heard it before, of course, and seen versions of it in advice-column headlines: 'How Soon Is Too Soon to U-Haul, Get Married, Have Ten Babies, Be Together Forever and Ever and Ever and Ever?'; 'To Be a U-Haul Lesbian or Not to Be a U-Haul Lesbian: Almost Definitely Not.' Most accounts trace the joke to comic Lea DeLaria, who inscribed the punchline into popular culture on *The Arsenio Hall Show* in the early 1990s. 'U-Haul lesbian' even has its own Wikipedia entry.

'This "urge to merge" had a basis in practicality in the 50s and early 60s, when gay couples had to remain in the shadows,' wrote Shauna Miller in the *Atlantic*. 'Back then, if you had the good fortune to make a family, you held onto it. It was a marriage. In the lesbian world, serial monogamy was safe, and also fulfilling. Women can have kids, too, so sometimes lesbians had those.'

The pattern stuck, or so the story goes. Where men stereotypically resist romantic commitment, women in same-sex relationships have long retained the reputation for getting too serious too fast, diving headfirst into domestic partnerships before they've established mutual compatibility.

'Lesbians have not had the benefit of cultural models telling them how [dating] is supposed to happen,' says Schwartz. As a result, she observes that many queer women find themselves in the romantic predicament of becoming deeply emotionally entwined with a partner who isn't a good long-term match. As members of a minority group where prospective partners may be scarce, this makes the prospect of breaking up – and staying broken up – incredibly daunting.

Maybe gender is a part of it, too. 'Women by nature try to maintain relational connections where they can,' offers a *Curve* magazine relationship advice columnist in an article titled 'How to Break Up with a Lesbian … Once.' Still, it seems that every few years a new study or argument is released that should, in theory, debunk our played-out preconceptions of how any gender experiences love.

The 2012 book *The Chemistry Between Us: Love, Sex, and the Science of Attraction*, written by neuroscientist Larry Young and science journalist Brian Alexander, put forth the argument that breakups are more difficult for men than they are for women. And a 2010 study published in the *Journal of Social Psychology* suggests that men fall in love faster and harder than women, even though both men and women are predisposed to believe the opposite is true. Its findings have resurfaced around Valentine's Day nearly every year since, easy clickbait for lovelorn singletons and flummoxed gender essentialists alike.

Same-sex couples may be at an advantage where it comes to processing their relationships' dissolutions, unencumbered by some of the weight of heteronormative baggage. 'Some straight women in my observation seem to have this kind of cynicism about men, where their breaking up becomes "Oh, he really was a jerk after all, just like the rest of them,"' says Schwartz. 'If you're a female with a female partner, it's harder to become cynical about women and write off the whole gender.'

Maybe writing off a whole gender is the easy way out of our conundrum, the purest act of agency in a mating ritual that positions women who partner with men as equal actors in a world that does not, in fact, materially reflect the values we uphold. I joke that heterosexuality is the karmic price I pay for my past life's sins, and I suspect I'm not alone in that sentiment. It's draining enough to do the work of loving without accounting for those unwieldy injustices beyond our control.

My younger self who so dreaded the unknown future would be pleased to see where I ended up. My present iteration frets less.

Relative security lightens the burden of choice. I lucked into a culture and class whose central invocation is a life of one's own choosing, but my greatest, least probable fortune came in somehow obtaining an adequate inflow of capital that would feasibly finance the dream. Where the formlessness of my life's eventual destination had once felt oppressive, I now understand it as a gift. My freedom to craft a life entirely in service of my personal will is a likely unprecedented privilege among my family's women, and one most women currently living will never have the unearned luxury of knowing firsthand.

If I sound optimistic, it's because I've yielded to the sybaritic thrall of false confidence. I could be laid off at any moment, and at some point I probably will be. I work in a fickle industry where even scalpel-sharp minds have been subject to closed-door meetings laying out their diminished labour market value. As many in my generation know too well, labour market value is a relative currency.

I earned my liberal arts degree mere months after the global market collapse of 2008. My final undergraduate year was so economically ominous that I couldn't even find a part-time job working retail or thawing hamburger patties for minimum wage – poverty-class employment that I felt indignantly entitled to. I'd spend most of the following year working sporadically or not at all, scavenging for babysitting gigs in between temp-agency placements and the odd, ill-suited contract. I moved in with my boyfriend my first post-grad winter, and he subsidized my share of the rent.

Though it seems that everyone these days identifies as a member of the middle class, those with the bank accounts to match the designation are the likeliest to tie the knot. Though I was born to middle-class parents, at the age of twenty-four I could not personally be counted among its ranks. It's possible that I would have been more decisive had my circumstances been different. Maybe I would have gotten married. Maybe I would have gone on a backpacking adventure and left my partner behind.

Today's dominant conversations about coupling and family formation orbit the gravitational entity of choice. Marriage is no longer a prerequisite for child-rearing, and child-rearing is no longer a given altogether. Even within the many subsets of society whose conservative values govern an adherence to a nuclear-family model, personal satisfaction is framed as the central facet of the package deal. Less often discussed is the reality of money: a political-economic structure that benefits dual-income households, and institutions designed to accommodate individuals ensconced in heterosexual domestic partnerships.

A 2011 study found that for every 1 per cent increase in the unemployment rate, the divorce rate proportionately goes down. This is not because unhappy couples somehow, in the face of adversity, rediscover their spark; on the contrary, nearly a quarter of the couples surveyed in the study reported that their relationships had become even worse, while a majority reported no change in either direction. But survival supersedes contentment. In exchange for economic security, people will endure marital strife.

The reasons why are obvious. Married couples continue to have a higher net worth than unmarried couples. Divorced couples fare worse than those who stay single,

Works Cited

1 Corinthians 7:5-6. Biblehub, 2016. http://biblehub.com/esv/1_corinthians/7.htm

Abbott, Elizabeth. *A History of Marriage: From Same Sex Unions to Private Vows and Common Law, the Surprising Diversity of Tradition*. New York, NY: Seven Stories Press, 2011.

Alexander, Brian. 'Why Breakups Are Harder on Men.' *Glamour*, April 4, 2016. https://www.glamour.com/story/why-breakups-are-harder-on-men-glamour-magazine-october-2012

Aslanian, Sasha. 'Divorced Kid: Stories from the 1970s Divorce Revolution.' American Public Media, January 3, 2010. https://divorcedkid.wordpress.com/a-divorce-revolution/

Bailey, Beth L. *From Front Porch to Back Seat: Courtship in Twentieth-Century America*. Baltimore, MD: Johns Hopkins University Press, 1989.

Balch, David L., and Carolyn Osiek. *Early Christian Families in Context: An Interdisciplinary Dialogue*. Grand Rapids, MI: William B. Eerdmans Pub, 2003.

Barker, Tess. 'How to Tell If You Should Break Up with That Nice Guy.' MTV, July 10, 2015. http://www.mtv.com/news/2204879/break-up-nice-guy/

Barrett, Michèle, and Kathi Weeks. *Women's Oppression Today: The Marxist/Feminist Encounter*. London: Verso Books, 2014.

Beauvoir, Simone de. *The Second Sex*. New York, NY: Vintage Books, 2011.

Bennett, John. *Letters to a Young Lady on a Variety of Useful and Interesting Subjects Calculated to Improve the Heart, to Form the Manners and to Enlighten the Understanding*. Warrington, UK: Hudson & Goodwin, 1798.

Behrendt, Greg, and Amiira Ruotola-Behrendt. *It's Called a Breakup Because It's Broken: The Smart Girl's Breakup Buddy*. New York, NY: Broadway Books, 2006.

Brown, Henry Box. Narrative of the Life of Henry Box Brown. United States: Andesite Press, 2015.

Cappellanus, Andreas. *The Art of Courtly Love*. Translated by J. J. Parry. New York, NY: W. W. Norton & Company, 1969.

Cauterucci, Christina. 'For Many Young Queer Women, *Lesbian* Offers a Fraught Inheritance.' *Slate*, December 20, 2016. http://www.slate.com/blogs/outward/2016/12/20/ young_queer_women_don_t_like_lesbian_as_a_name_here_s_why.html

———. 'More Unmarried Americans than Ever Are Cohabiting.' *Slate*, April 7, 2017. http://www.slate.com/blogs/xx_factor/2017/04/07/more_unmarried_americans_than_ever_are_cohabitating.html

Celello, Kristin, and Hanan Kholoussy, eds. *Domestic Tensions, National Anxieties: Global Perspectives on Marriage, Crisis, and Nation*. New York, NY: Oxford University Press, 2016.

Chambers, Anne Lorene. '"If the Laws Were Made More Salutary": The Act of 1859.' *Married Women and Property Law in Victorian Ontario*, 70-91.

Toronto, ON: University of Toronto Press, 1997. doi:www.jstor.org/stable/10.3138/9781442677098.9.

Cheever, George Barrell, et al. *Memorabilia of George B. Cheever, D.D., Late Pastor of the Church of the Puritans, Union Square, New York, and of His Wife Elizabeth Wetmore Cheever in Verse and Prose*. New York, NY: Wiley, 1890.

Chen, Michelle. 'Women Owe Two-thirds of Student Loan Debt. This Points to a Slow-burning Crisis.' *The Guardian*, June 21, 2017. https://www.theguardian.com/commentisfree/2017/jun/21/women-two-thirds-student-loan-debt-slow-burning-crisis

Cherlin, Andrew J. *The Marriage-Go-Round: The State of Marriage and the Family in America Today*. New York, NY: Vintage Books, 2010.

Chernock, Arianne. *Men and the Making of Modern British Feminism*. Stanford, CA: Stanford University Press, 2010.

Clement, Elizabeth Alice. *Love for Sale: Courting, Treating, and Prostitution in New York City, 1900-1945*. Chapel Hill, NC: University of North Carolina Press, 2006.

Cody, Cheryll Ann. 'Sale and Separation: Four Crises for Enslaved Women on the Ball Plantations, 1764–1854.' In *Working toward Freedom: Slave Society and Domestic Economy in the American South*, edited by Larry E. Hudson, 119-139. Rochester, NY: University of Rochester Press, 1994.

Cohen, M. 'Women and the Progressive Movement.' Gilder Lehrman Institute of American History, 2012. https://www.gilderlehrman.org/history-by-era/politics-reform/essays/women-and-progressive-movement

Conley, T. D., et al. 'Investigation of Consensually Nonmonogamous Relationships.' *Perspectives on Psychological Science*, 12, no. 2, (2017): 205-232. doi:10.1177/1745691616667925

Coontz, Stephanie. *Marriage, a History: How Love Conquered Marriage*. New York, NY: Penguin Group, 2006.

———. *A Strange Stirring: 'The Feminine Mystique' and American Women at the Dawn of the 1960s*. New York, NY: Basic Books, 2012.

Davis, Rebecca L. '"Not Marriage at All, but Simple Harlotry": The Companionate Marriage Controversy.' *Journal of American History*, 94, no. 4 (2008): 1137-1163. doi:10.2307/25095323

Dodge, Grace H. 'Glimpses into the Lives of Working-Women.' *Harper's Bazaar*, 4th ed., vol. 23 (1890).

Donevan, Connor. 'Millennials Navigate the Ups and Downs of Cohabitation.' NPR, November 1, 2014. http://www.npr.org/2014/11/01/358876955/millennials-navigate-the-ups-and-downs-of-cohabitation

Dreiser, Theodore. *Sister Carrie*. New York: Doubleday, Page, 1970.

Eby, Clare Virginia. *Until Choice Do Us Part: Marriage Reform in the Progressive Era*. Chicago, IL: University of Chicago Press, 2014.

Elder, G. H. 'Appearance and Education in Marriage Mobility.' *American Sociological Review*, 34, no. 4 (1969): 519. doi:10.2307/2091961

Encyclopædia Britannica. 'Seminole Wars.' Accessed July 21, 2016. https://www.britannica.com/topic/Seminole-Wars

Engels, Friedrich, and Ernest Untermann. *The Origin of the Family: Private Property and the State*. Chicago, IL: Charles H. Kerr & Company Co-operative, 1902.

Finkelman, Paul. 'Scott V. Sandford: The Court's Most Dreadful Case and How It Changed History.' *Chicago-Kent Law Review*, 82, (2006): 3-48. https://scholarship.kentlaw.iit.edu/cgi/viewcontent.cgi?referer=&httpsredir=1&article=3570&context=cklawreview

Firestone, Shulamith. *The Dialectic of Sex: The Case for Feminist Revolution*. London: Verso Books, 2015.

Fitzgerald, F. Scott. *This Side of Paradise*. New York, NY: Penguin Classics, 1996.

'The "Flapper" Has Her Turn.' *New York Times*, February 8, 1918. https://timesmachine.nytimes.com/timesmachine/1917/02/08/issue.html

Friedan, Betty. *The Feminine Mystique*. New York, NY: W. W. Norton & Company, 2013.

Galatians 5:16-17. *New International Version*. Colorado Springs, CO: Biblica, 2011. biblehub.com.

Gardner, Richard A. *The Boys and Girls Book about Divorce*. New York, NY: Bantam Books, 1985.

Gibson, Campbell, and Kay Jung. 'Historical Census Statistics on the Foreign-Born Population of the United States: 1850–2000.' *Working Paper No. 81*. Washington, D.C.: Population Division, US Census Bureau, 2006. https://www.census.gov/population/www/documentation/twps0081/twps0081.html

Gies, Frances and Joseph. *Marriage and the Family in the Middle Ages*. New York, NY: Harper & Row, 2000.

Goldin, Claudia. 'The Female Labor Force and American Economic Growth, 1890–1980.' In *Long-Term Factors in American Economic Growth*, edited by Stanley L. Engerman and Robert E. Gallman, 557-604. Chicago, IL: University of Chicago Press, 1986. doi:http://www.nber.org/chapters/ c9688.pdf

——'Gender Gap.' In *The Concise Encyclopedia of Economics*, 2002. http://www.econlib.org/library/Enc1/GenderGap.html

—— 'The Work and Wages of Single Women, 1870 to 1920.' *Journal of Economic History*, 40, no. 1 (1980): 81-88. doi:10.1017/s0022050700104565

Goldman, Emma. 'The Traffic in Women.' *Anarchism and Other Essays*. New York, NY: Dover Publications, 1969.

Goring, Darlene. 'The History of Slave Marriage in the United States.' *Louisiana State University Law Center* (2006): 299-347. https://digitalcommons.law.lsu.edu/cgi/viewcontent.cgi?referer=&httpsredir=1&article=1262&context=faculty_scholarship

Government of Canada, Dept of Finance. 'The Political Economy of Student Debt in Canada.' March 2017. http://cfs-fcee.ca/wp-content/uploads/sites/71/2017/04/PESD-Booklayout-final.pdf

Grand, Sarah. 'The New Aspect of the Woman Question.' *North American Review*, 158, no. 448 (1894): 270-276. https://www.jstor.org/stable/25103291

Grant, Tavia. 'Statistics Canada to Stop Tracking Marriage and Divorce Rates.' *The Globe and Mail*, July 20, 2011.

Gray, John. *Beyond Mars and Venus: Relationship Skills for Today's Complex World*. Dallas, TX: BenBella Books, 2017.

Greenstone, Michael, and Adam Looney. 'The Marriage Gap: The Impact of Economic and Technological Change on Marriage Rates.' Hamilton Project, February 2, 2012. http://www.hamiltonproject.org/papers/the_ marriage_gap_the_impact_of_economic_and_technological_change_on_ma

Hamilton, G. V. *A Research in Marriage*. New York, NY: A & C Boni, 1929.

Handel, Peter. '50th Anniversary of "The Feminine Mystique": Friedan's Rediscovered Writings on Industrial Working Women.' *Truthout*, July 21, 2013. http://www.truth-out.org/opinion/item/17581-50th-anniversary-of-the-feminine-mystique-friedans-rediscovered-writings-on-industrial-working-women

Harrison, Marissa A., and Jennifer C. Shortall. 'Women and Men in Love: Who Really Feels It and Says It First?' *Journal of Social Psychology*, 151, no. 6 (2011): 727-736. doi:10.1080/00224545.2010.522626

'Have You Ever Broken Up with a Good Guy?' Reddit, August 30, 2015. https://www.reddit.com/r/AskWomen/comments/3iykd3/have_you_ever_broken_up_with_a_good_guy

Hawes, Joseph M., and Elizabeth F. Shores. *The Family in America: An Encyclopedia*, Vol. 2: 799. Santa Barbara, CA: ABC-CLIO, 2001.

Heckel, N. *Sex, Society and Medieval Women*. University of Rochester Libraries, n.d. https://www.library.rochester.edu/robbins/sexsociety#eleanor

Henry, Ben. 'Beyoncé Is Pregnant and Celebrities Are Just as Excited as We Are.' Buzzfeed, February 2, 2017. https://www.buzzfeed.com/benhenry/congrats-to-my-best-friend-beyonce

Hill, Shirley A. 'Marriage among African American Women: A Gender Perspective.' *Journal of Comparative Family Studies*, 37, no. 3 (2006): 428-428. http://www.jstor.org/stable/41604091?seq=1#page_scan_tab_contents

Hine, Robert V., John Mack Faragher, and Jon T. Coleman. 'The Urban Frontier.' *The American West: A New Interpretive History*. New Haven, CT: Yale University Press, 2000.

hooks, bell. *Feminist Theory: From Margin to Center*. 2nd ed. Cabridge, MA: South End Press, 2000.

Horowitz, David. 'Rethinking Betty Friedan and *The Feminine Mystique*: Labor Union Radicalism and Feminism in Cold War America.' *American Quarterly*, 48, no. 1 (1996): 1-42. doi:10.1353/aq.1996.0010

Hunt, Alan. *Governing Morals: A Social History of Moral Regulation*. Cambridge, UK: Cambridge University Press, 2009.

Hunter, Tera W. 'Putting an Antebellum Myth to Rest.' *New York Times*, August 2, 2011. http://www.nytimes.com/2011/08/02/opinion/putting-an-antebellum-myth-about-slave-families-to-rest.html

———. *Bound in Wedlock: Slave and Free Black Marriage in the Nineteenth Century*. Cambridge, MA: The Belknap Press of Harvard University Press, 2017.

———. 'Slave Marriages, Families Were Often Shattered by Auction Block.' By Michel Martin. New Discoveries in Black History. NPR, February 11, 2010.

Ireton, Julie and Josh Bloch. 'How Two Friends Fought to Be Legal "Co-mommas" to a 7-Year-Old Boy – and Won.' *The Current*. CBC Radio, February 21, 2017. http://www.cbc.ca/radio/thecurrent/the-current-for-february-21-2017-1.3991287/how-two-friends-fought-to-be-legal-co-mommas-to-a-7-year-old-boy-and-won-1.3991307

Isen, Adam, and Betsey Stevenson. 'Women's Education and Family Behavior: Trends in Marriage, Divorce and Fertility.' NBER Working Paper No. 15725, 2010. doi:10.3386/w15725

'Jean-Martin Charcot: 1825–1893.' *A Science Odyssey: People and Discoveries*. PBS, 1998. http://www.pbs.org/wgbh/aso/databank/entries/bhchar.html

Jones, Hazel. *Jane Austen and Marriage*. New York, NY: Continuum International Publishing Group, 2009.

Juster, Norton. *A Woman's Place: Yesterday's Women in Rural America*. Golden, CO: Fulcrum Pub, 1996.

Katz, William Loren. *Black Indians: A Hidden Heritage*. New York, NY: Atheneum Books for Young Readers, 2012.

Keith, Thomas. *Masculinities in Contemporary American Culture: An Intersectional Approach to the Complexities and Challenges of Male Identity*. Basingstoke: Taylor & Francis, 2016.

Kessler-Harris, Alice. *Out to Work: A History of Wage-Earning Women in the United States*. Oxford, UK: Oxford University Press, 1982.

Wattenberg, Ben. 'Alice Kessler-Harris Interview.' *The First Measured Century*. PBS, n.d. https://www.pbs.org/fmc/interviews/kesslerharris.htm

Khan, B. Zorina. *The Democratization of Invention: Patents and Copyrights in American Economic Development, 1790–1920*. Cambridge, UK: Cambridge University Press, 2009.

Laselle, Mary A. *The Young Woman Worker*. Boston, MA: Pilgrim Press, 1914.

Lavietes, Stuart. 'Richard Gardner, 72, Dies; Cast Doubt on Abuse Claims.' *New York Times*, June 8, 2003. http://www.nytimes.com/2003/06/09/nyregion/richard-gardner-72-dies-cast-doubt-on-abuse-claims.html

Law Library of Congress. 'Married Women's Property Laws.' American Women. https://memory.loc.gov/ammem/awhhtml/awlaw3/property_law.html

'Learn About Mutual Arrangements.' SeekingArrangement. https://www.seekingarrangement.com/what-is-an-arrangement

Lifflander, Matthew L. 'The Tragedy That Changed New York.' *New York Archives*, 2011. https://www.sutori.com/item/the-triangle-shirtwaist-factory-catches-fire-march-25-1911-the-tr

Linn, Allison. 'Why Married People Tend to Be Wealthier: It's Complicated.' *Today*, February 13, 2013. https://www.today.com/money/why-married-people-tend-be-wealthier-its-complicated-1C8364877

Lorde, Audre. 'Age, Race, Class, and Sex.' *Sister Outsider: Essays and Speeches*. New York, NY: Crown Publishing, 1984.

Low, Corinne. *Essays in Gender Economics*. New York, NY: Columbia University Academic Commons, 2014. doi: https://academiccommons.columbia.edu/catalog/ac:175735

MacFarlane, Alan. *The Culture of Capitalism*. Oxford, UK: B. Blackwell, 1989.

Magoun, Horace Winchell, and Louise H. Marshall. *American Neuroscience in the Twentieth Century: Confluence of the Neural, Behavioral, and the Communicative Streams*. London, UK: Swets and Zeitlinger, 2003.

Mandel, E. M. 'A Flapper Speaks.' *New York Times*, December 31, 1921. https://timesmachine.nytimes.com/timesmachine/1921/12/31/98780616.html

Martin, Rachel. 'Sorting Through the Numbers on Infidelity.' NPR, July 26, 2015. http://www.npr.org/2015/07/26/426434619/sorting-through-the-numbers-on-infidelity

Mayer, Alyx. 'Capitalist Sexuality and "Sex-Positive Feminism."' Anti-Imperialism, February 23, 2017. https://anti-imperialism.org/2016/07/11/capitalist-sexuality-and-sex-positive-feminism

McDermott, John. 'Why Conservatives Think the Gender Pay Gap Is a "Myth."' *Mel*, April 28, 2017. https://melmagazine.com/why-conservatives-think-the-gender-gap-is-a-myth-7b0c604d6409

Menand, Louis. 'Books as Bombs.' *New Yorker*, January 24, 2011. http://www.newyorker.com/magazine/2011/01/24/books-as-bombs

Miller, Kevin. 'The Simple Truth about the Gender Pay Gap.' American Association of University Women, 2017. http://www.aauw.org/research/the-simple-truth-about-the-gender-pay-gap

Miller, Shauna. 'Beyond the U-Haul: How Lesbian Relationships Are Changing.' *The Atlantic*, July 3, 2013. https://www.theatlantic.com/sexes/archive/2013/07/beyond-the-u-haul-how-lesbian-relationships-are-changing/277495

Mintz, Steven, and Susan Kellogg. *Domestic Revolutions: A Social History of American Family Life*. New York, NY: Free Press, 1989.

MissPredicament. 'PSA: You can break up with someone for any reason, or for no reason at all. You don't have to have a "good reason" to end a relationship.' Reddit, September 13, 2015. https://www.reddit.com/r/TwoXChromosomes/comments/3ktwrh/psa_you_can_break_up_with_someone_fo r_any_reason

Moore, Fhionna, Clare Cassidy, and David I. Perrett. 'The Effects of Control of Resources on Magnitudes of Sex Differences in Human Mate Preferences.' *Evolutionary Psychology*, 8, no. 4 (2010). doi:10.1177/147470491000800412

Moore, Lane, and Cosmo Frank. '9 Things Guys Think Are Romantic, but Aren't.' *Cosmopolitan*, July 21, 2015. http://www.cosmopolitan.com/sex-love/news/a44155/things-guys-think-are-romantic-but-arent

Moyser, Melissa. 'Women and Paid Work.' Statistics Canada, March 9, 2017. http://www.statcan.gc.ca/pub/89-503-x/2015001/article/14694-eng.htm

Natash. 'How to Break Up with a Lesbian … Once.' *Curve*, January 15, 2016 . http://www.curvemag.com/Advice/How-to-Break-Up-with-a-Lesbian Once-877

Norman, Martha Prescod. 'Shining in the Dark: Black Women and the Struggle for the Vote, 1955–1965.' In *African American Women and the Vote, 1837–1965*. Edited by Ann D. Gordon and Bettye Collier-Thomas. Amherst: University of Massachusetts Press, 1997.

O'Brien, Elizabeth. 'Marriage Is Good for Couples' Finances: Are You and Your Spouse on the Right Track?' *Time*, August 23, 2016. http://time.com/money/4455829/marriage-good-for-couples-finances-tell-your-story

O'Leary, Margaret. 'More Ado about the Flapper.' *New York Times*, April 16, 1922. https://timesmachine.nytimes.com/timesmachine/1922/04/16/107051068.html

Ovid. *The Love Books of Ovid Being the Amores, Ars Amatoria, Remedia Amoris and Medicamina Faciei Femineae of Publius Ovidius Naso*. Translated by David R. Slavitt. Whitefish, MT: Kessinger Publishing, 2005.

Plutarch. *Plutarch's Lives*. Translated by John Langhorne and William Langhorne. Baltimore, MD: William & Joseph Neal, 1834.

Packard, Vance. 'The Ad and the Id.' *Harper's Bazaar*, August 1957. http://ezproxy.nypl.org/login?url=https://search.proquest.com/docview/1832461330?accountid=35635

Patton, Holly. 'The Hardest Break-up I Ever Had Was with a Nice Guy.' Hello Giggles, August 12, 2015. http://hellogiggles.com/break-up-nice-guy/

Peale, Norman Vincent. *The Power of Positive Thinking*. New York, NY: Touchstone/Simon & Schuster, 2015.

Peiss, Kathy. *Cheap Amusements: Working Women and Leisure in Turn-of-the-Century New York*. Philadelphia, PA: Temple University Press, 1986.

Pew Research Center. 'The Decline of Marriage and Rise of New Families.' *Social and Demographic Trends*, November 17, 2010. http://www.pewsocialtrends.org/2010/11/18/the-decline-of-marriage-and-rise-of-new- families

———. 'The New American Father.' *Social and Demographic Trends*, June 14, 2013. http://www.pewsocialtrends.org/2013/06/14/the-new-american-father

———. 'Record Share of Americans Have Never Married.' *Social and Demographic Trends*, September 23, 2014. http://www.pewsocialtrends.org/2014/09/24/record-share-of-americans-have-never-married/#will-todays-never-married-adults-eventually-marry

———. 'Gay Marriage Around the World.' *Religion & Public Life*, August 7, 2017. http://www.pewforum.org/2017/06/30/gay-marriage-around-the-world-2013/#us

———. '5 Facts on Love and Marriage in America.' *FactTank*, February 13, 2017. http://www.pewresearch.org/fact-tank/2017/02/13/5-facts-about-love-and-marriage

and Consumer Issues, 13, no. 1 (2008). https://projects.ncsu.edu/ffci/
publications/2008/v13-n1-2008-spring/Washburn-Christensen.php

'Wedding Services in the US: Market Research Report.' IbisWorld, August
2017. https://www.ibisworld.com/industry-trends/market-research-
reports/other-services-except-public-administration/repair-
maintenance/wedding-services.html

Weigel, Moira. *Labor of Love: The Invention of Dating*. New York, NY: Farrar,
Straus & Giroux, 2016.

West, Emily. 'Surviving Separation: Cross-Plantation Marriages and the Slave
Trade in Antebellum South Carolina.' *Journal of Family History*, 24, no. 2
(1999): 215. http://journals.sagepub.com/doi/abs/10.1177/
036319909902400205

White, Helen McCann. 'Guide to a Microfilm Edition of The Lawrence Taliaferro Papers.' Minnesota Historical Society, 1966. doi:http://www2.mnhs.
org/library/findaids/m0035.pdf

Wilcox, W. Bradford. 'The Evolution of Divorce.' *National Affairs*, Fall 2009.
http://www.nationalaffairs.com/publications/detail/the-evolution-of-
divorce

Will, Thomas E. 'Weddings on Contested Grounds: Slave Marriage in the Antebellum South.' *Historian*, 62, no. 1 (1999): 99-117. http://onlinelibrary.
wiley.com/doi/10.1111/j.1540-6563.1999.tb01436.x/full

Wollstonecraft, Mary. *A Vindication of the Rights of Women*. Project Gutenberg, 2001. https://www.marxists.org/reference/archive/wollstonecraft-
mary/1792/vindication-rights-woman/ch04.htm

Woolf, Virginia. *A Room of One's Own*. Oxford, UK: Blackwell, 1992.

Young, Larry, and Brian Alexander. *The Chemistry Between Us: Love, Sex, and
the Science of Attraction*. New York, NY: Current, 2014.

Zeitz, Joshua. *Flapper: A Madcap Story of Sex, Style, Celebrity, and the Women
Who Made America Modern*. New York, NY: Three Rivers Press, 2006.

Acknowledgements

Like so many good things, a book is a group effort. This project simply would not have happened without the guiding insight of my editor, friend, and eternal champion Emily M. Keeler, whose mind is an international treasure. If only every single book could be edited by Emily. Many heaps of thanks also go to Alana Wilcox and the Coach House team, who generously took a chance on this idea and have ushered it to fruition with utmost wisdom, enthusiasm, and, most especially, patience. I'm a lucky woman.

I've been fortunate to have the support and encouragement of many good people along the way, both during the process of writing and in the course of events that led to it. Special thanks go to Carmen Price, Lisan Jutras, Naben Ruthnum, Danielle Liebowitz, Laura-Louise Tobin, Jon Medow, Shawn Micallef, Hamutal Dotan, Sarah Barmak, Alex Molotkow, Ruby Brunton, Heather Zayde, Tabatha Southey, Carly Fisher, Greylord and Julio, my Brit + Co crew, and to Ivor Tossell, my first reader and hand-holder and dinner-feeder, for continuing to give me cause to hold my nose and proceed with the conventions of love.

Finally, a special thanks to my family – especially my parents, Rick and Marina, and my brothers Casey and Ricky.

Kelli María Korducki is a journalist and cultural critic. Her byline has appeared frequently in the *Globe and Mail* and *National Post*, as well as in the *New Inquiry*, NPR, the *Walrus*, *Vice*, and the *Hairpin*. She was nominated for a 2015 National Magazine Award for 'Tiny Triumphs,' a 10,000-word meditation on the humble hot dog for *Little Brother*. A former editor-in-chief of the popular daily news blog *The Torontoist*, Korducki is based in Toronto and Brooklyn.

About the
Exploded Views Series

Exploded Views is a series of probing, provocative essays that offer surprising perspectives on the most intriguing cultural issues and figures of our day. Longer than a typical magazine article but shorter than a full-length book, these are punchy salvos written by some of North America's most lyrical journalists and critics. Spanning a variety of forms and genres – history, biography, polemic, commentary – and published simultaneously in all digital formats and handsome, collectible print editions, this is literary reportage that at once investigates, illuminates, and intervenes.

www.chbooks.com/explodedviews

Typeset in Goodchild Pro and Gibson Pro. Goodchild was designed by Nick Shinn in 2002 at his ShinnType foundry in Orangeville, Ontario. Shinn's design takes its inspiration from French printer Nicholas Jenson who, at the height of the Renaissance in Venice, used the basic Carolingian minuscule calligraphic hand and classic roman inscriptional capitals to arrive at a typeface that produced a clear and even texture that most literate Europeans could read. Shinn's design captures the calligraphic feel of Jensen's early types in a more refined digital format. Gibson was designed by Rod McDonald in honour of John Gibson FGDC (1928–2011), Rod's long-time friend and one of the founders of the Society of Graphic Designers of Canada. It was McDonald's intention to design a solid, contemporary, and affordable sans serif face.

Printed at the old Coach House on bpNichol Lane in Toronto, Ontario, on Rolland Opaque Natural paper, which was manufactured, acid-free, in Saint-Jérôme, Quebec, from 50 per cent recycled paper, and it was printed with vegetable-based ink on a 1972 Heidelberg KORD offset litho press. Its pages were folded on a Baumfolder, gathered by hand, bound on a Sulby Auto-Minabinda, and trimmed on a Polar single-knife cutter.

Series editor: Emily M. Keeler
Cover illustration by Chloe Cushman
Author photo by Laurel Golio

Coach House Books
80 bpNichol Lane
Toronto ON M5S 3J4
Canada

416 979 2217
800 367 6360

mail@chbooks.com
www.chbooks.com